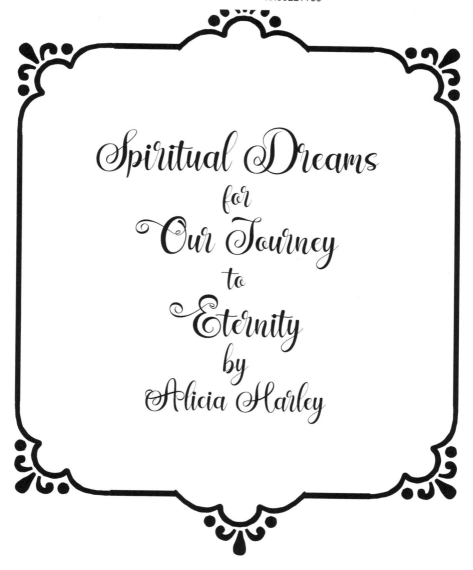

Spiritual Dreams
for
Our Journey
to
Eternity
by
Alicia Harley

Spiritual Dreams for Our Journey to Eternity
by Alicia Harley

Designed and published by Goodbooks Media

Printed in the U.S.A.

ISBN: 9798368180595

goodbooks
GOODBOOKS MEDIA
3453 Aransas
Corpus Christi, Texas, 78411
goodbooksmedia.com

Table of Contents

Preface
by
Dr. Ronda Chervin

I met Alicia Harley at a series of talks I gave about Teresa of Avila's Interior Castle. She stood out because she is beautiful, intense, and radiates eagerness to learn.

During the talks I would sometimes ask if anyone in the group had experienced similar graces to those St. Teresa wrote about. Alicia was one of the few who would respond.

When the sessions ended, she began to tell me about some of her dreams. Unfamiliar with the theology of spirituality, Alicia wasn't aware that "dreams" of the type she often had are what is called "interior visions."

An interior vision is not seen as outside the recipient's body as, say, in the case of apparitions. It is like an interior locution, sometimes called "a word in the heart," which is not heard with the ears, but "listened to" within the soul. The "interior vision" is like a dream but its content is not a fantastic jumble of images. It is a coherent series of pictures with a spiritual theme.

Now, when a recipient of such interior visions tells a priest or some other spiritual mentor about such happenings, the mentor is always cautious. After all, if everyone believed everything they saw in such dreams or heard in such locutions, evil spirits could mislead anyone at any time.

However, in Alicia's case, the priests she spoke to never thought these many dreams were coming from evil spirits.

Since I have written many books about Catholic spirituality and the saints, I asked Alicia to show me some of the pages she had compiled of such dreams. Never did they seem to me to be from evil spirits. Instead, each one seemed to me to convey Catholic truths in the form of vivid imagery.

I suggested that Alicia put them together in the book that is now in your hands.

As I was reading Alicia's dreams, I commented on how I would apply what I thought was a meaning of a dream to my own spiritual life.

This morphed into the idea of adding such comments at the bottom of the last paper of each dream. This will help the reader relate to the messages.

Acknowledgment

I acknowledge the Alpha and Omega, the Supreme Being and the 'I AM' as the perfection to all that is and will be throughout eternity and I worship in gratitude for whom He is: The Father, Son and Holy Spirit. As he gave us the most precious gift of all, Our Lord the Savior, The Salvation of the World, Our Lord Jesus Christ upon the cross and through the institution of the Holy Eucharist in the Catholic church. Thank God, always for there are no Gods before thee!

Thank you to my three children: Kristian Faith Lopez, Theresa Marie Lopez and Douglas H. Harley. Also, thank you to my wonderful husband, Douglas W. Harley. I love you and consider all of you wonderful gifts from God.

Thank you to Dr. Ronda Chervin for being my good Catholic friend and Mentor. Thank you, Jim, my publisher for loving the dreams or interior visions.

God bless you my friends!

Prologue

Before telling you about my dreams or interior visions, as a child, a married woman and mother, a word about my background. Dreaming of the spiritual world is normal to me and I thought it was something everyone dreams did. However, I found that not to be true as I became an adult married with adult children. It took me a long time to figure out that my dreams are more than dreams and not considered actual dreams, in the ordinary sense and that word. So, I thought it is time to allow others to journey with me into this spiritual world of dreams or now known to be interior visions.

I started to question people on occasion, even posting on Facebook, "Do you dream this way?" or "Feel Like Sharing..." The response is not what I wanted to hear. It was usually "No." So, the best thing was that I ventured out to the confessional to discuss my dreams with a priest one day. I told the priest about a spiritual dream. He found the dream interesting, but he said, "It is not a dream!" and told me, "Write down your dreams with a time and date."

In obedience, I followed the priest's advice, and it has been a huge blessing to write them down. Spiritual dreams I remember having prior to writing them down will be marked as 'No Date' because they will be strictly, as I remember them before I received a blessing and the idea from a priest to write them down.

You may say, "Well it may be easy for you to dream this way or about spiritual things if your upbring was in a religious family?" False! You could have no religion in your youth and later in life recognize that a faith-based life is of the uttermost importance. The Holy Spirit taps people into the spiritual realm. When a person has a strong prayer life and recognizes Jesus Christ, as Lord and Savior, then, the spiritual realm intensifies in the person. But the "Why Me and not you or you and not some others?" becomes the difficult question for there may never be an answer. The 'Why' is something a person like me must learn to embrace and quit asking it? Move on…

Here is a sample of one of my dreams so you can get a sense of what they are like:

Chapter Eight

Dream of Extreme Poverty

September 06, 2012

It was an unusual large place where nuns were staying with children. A nun told me, "I am Sister Teresa."

She added, "I am going to leave to attend to the poorest of the poorest. Take me there! I told her, "Yes" and together we walked out of the large building.

However, I told her to wait up for me because she had left all her important items behind, so I went back inside the building. Now, the building took a change, it was quite different and not at all a normal room. It was very elegant. I saw beautiful furniture, cushions with carpet from one area to the next. So, I looked around and started walking back outside of the room.

As I stepped outside the door of the building, I saw passengers on a train, and it was children without their parents sitting in a cargo of a train looking out the window. The young children were about seven to eleven years of age. The children had dirty hair and clothing that was torn up.

A fire engine followed the train, which I thought was an unusual thing to see in my dream. So, I started to walk and saw a pile of ashes. The ashes were high and smoldering, just like in a fireplace. I got close to the ashes to see what was on top of the ashes. It was a cross.

I saw a large wooden cross with the Infant Jesus laying on top of the cross. The cross He was on was laying on top of the ashes. I stood there looking at Him because He started to move slightly, as if He was in severe pain. The Infant Jesus in agony was moving on the wooden cross He looked at me and spoke in a command, "Go and find someone to come and help, and be with Me!"

Just so you can picture me, a wife, mother, a previous GED college instructor and now at this moment writing about dreams of the spiritual world. Let's start this journey at the very beginning of these roles.

Personal Background

For example, I was born into a Catholic family in Corpus Christi, Texas. But my family did not attend Sunday Mass. However, they made sure I did get my sacraments through the church by taking me, as a young child to religion classes. They planted the seed of faith even though it was up to me to figure out what was true. The danger was that I could have easily gotten lost in this great big world.

However, the opposite happened, I did have lots of love from loving parents and family members. Yes, a child can see love and wants to reciprocate it slowly as it grows up in life.

My Parents

Both of my parents, mother and father were illiterate in

both English and Spanish. They could not read or write in either language. Education at that time was unattainable in the farms where they lived in South Texas. My parents met and married in Corpus Christi, Texas. They were married in a traditional Catholic wedding at St. Joseph's Catholic church in the mid-nineteen sixties. The difficulty for my father was not the problem of being able to find a job when a current job ended, as he was in construction. His problem was his lack of literacy skills.

Imagine filling out job applications! Since my dad was unable to read and write, he would bring home the applications for me to fill out for him. I was sure if my father had only one wish it would be for him to know how to read and write.

His own dream became a simple one, "I want my daughter to get a high school education" and even, miraculously, to one day go to college. It became obvious when he showed up at my high school counselor's office unannounced one day. My father sat with me and the counselor to reassure himself that I had all the credits necessary to graduate high school.

I lost sight of my own graduation, when waving out to him in a crowd of spectators I realized it was not about me but about my father's overcoming fear of failure in education and parenting. Furthermore, the moment of my high school graduation was a huge gain of optimism in the future generations to come. It was a great parental goal that became the dream come true of a simple man.

Now going back to my younger years, I saw this glimpse of God. During my high school years, I attended a Bible class with other young adults my age. The class, taught by an older woman of Jewish descent, brought the Bible to life. As, a high school student I read the entire Old Testament and

Genealogy of the Bible. I found delight in reading the Bible, as I really was not an avid reader before, but this time it was different. It is a treasure to the mind and soul! It opened my spirit up to God. The Bible used in my high schools' years purchased at a thrift store for a couple of cents. I consider it a grace waiting for me on the shelf of the store. I wrote on the Bible and took notes on it in class. The Bible from high school is still within my home library. It has been read and accessed by my children in their beginnings of religious educational classes. As a high schooler at that time, it was the best time because happiness, faith and true love found me. It was heaven! God was already reaching out to me, and I was listening to him.

At that time, my parents' marriage was collapsing. For many years, my father was single. Later in his elder years, he would marry, as he found happiness and love with a nice lady.

After I graduated from high school, I went to a local community college; however, my father's dream was for me to become a lawyer. So much was he on keen on me becoming a lawyer that he would take me to the office of a few lawyers to talk about careers in law. But I was not interested in becoming a lawyer.

When my parents divorced, my father and I did not speak for months. Mostly, he became upset at the realization that I would never go to law school. So, his stress built up as he was unsure of how life would embrace this young girl in the future. But what he did not know is I had found something deeply profound, and it built a solid foundation within my soul.

God Sends an "Expert of the Experts" My Way

It is God, the builder who gently, slowly, and patiently

handed me pieces of the puzzle even in dreams. Looking back, He was giving me a chance to figure it out or to try putting together the pieces of the puzzle through mystical dreams. Upon waking I often see the dreams as insights or glimpses of God's ways and His love for all.

As you will see in the chapters of dreams, there are teaching dreams, demonic dreams and more of them the good angel dreams. I thought I was strange and kept it quiet until February 29, 2020. This dream which is written into chapter thirty-three changed my life forever and I instinctively knew it was not normal to dream this way.

However, I turned to God in the adoration chapel one day after dreaming the dream from chapter thirty-three and begged God to help me. I asked him, "It is wonderful to write these dreams down but what I am supposed to do with them? Honestly, I would like to write a book, but I do not have the slightest idea where to even start or what to do. If you would want me to write a book, then please help me with it! For I have no idea on what to do or how to even start writing a book." So, I called out to God in prayer within the adoration chapel for about two hours.

One day and several months later, God sent as I call her an 'Expert of the Experts' my way just a couple of blocks away from my home within walking distance to St. John's Catholic Church. This is where I met Dr. Ronda Chervin, as she was teaching a class on a saint. She has written over sixty books on saints and religion. After attending her session, I spoke to her about my dreams. Dr. Chervin insisted on seeing the writings on the dreams and came over to my home. After viewing the dreams and speaking to me for a while, over time, this Professor of Philosophy and International Speaker who taught many priest throughout the world would soon reveal and tell me, "These are not dreams. Your dreams are what is known as "Interior Visions.""

Formation of a Young Child into an Adult

Now, I will take this opportunity to comment on my formation as a person. I do remember how hard my family made sure I learned good morals of being polite and respectful towards people. Even a great priest gave the advice, "Remember, just respect yourself!" Respect builds character with moral values. If we respect ourselves, one will truly know who we are in life. Respect will knock out the chatter, confusion, and noise. We will listen to ourselves with wisdom no matter what age we are or the situation we find ourselves. We will be guided into the area of light and wisdom even in demanding situations in life even though you may not see it at the precise moment.

Later in life, I took a slice out of the golden pie labeled 'Respect' and lovingly conveyed it with the heart to my own children, as they attended school in their elementary years. 'Show-and-Tell' took place, as I would always make sure to tell other parents and adults in front of my children, "Mr. or Mrs., etc.," so they would understand how to show respect for their elders in their speech. It became a habit. The funny thing the habit became so evident that I would address my peers at times in the same manner when my children were not around me. Sometimes I would catch myself addressing other parents this way. However, my kids later as adults learned it was okay to call other adults by their first name.

What kept my childhood family together was a simple and humble thing called LOVE. The bond of my aunt on the maternal side of the family brought hope to the eyes of a single parent raising daughters. One of my mother's sisters, my beloved aunt along with their siblings put great emphasis of appropriate behavior and sheltered me from the dangers of the outside world. Being a very sheltered child there were no sleep overs at friends' home except for my young cousin's homes, otherwise it was not allowable!

My aunt took sole responsibility of my mother, since my mother had been a sick child. She took the role of a mother. Now my mother, a simple woman with beautiful authentic natural looks was naïve about the outside world of hard work or even paying bills. This was due to a highly sheltered life.

However, I remember her gentle and kind voice singing Spanish lullabies to help me fall asleep. The reason for her sheltered life: tuberculosis. Yes, my mother was a victim of a horrible disease at the youthful age of fifteen. She was left with a large visible incision on her back due to life saving measures which required surgery.

She was a beautiful young child who one day got sick after playing outside on a sweltering day. They discovered her disease after she had severe fatigue and fevers. After seeking medical treatment in Houston, the financial burden became a strain within her family of seven sisters and one brother, but they all succeeded in doing their absolute best in assisting her to have a good outcome in this medical ordeal.

One of my mother's sisters sacrificed herself for the sake of love and took it upon herself to raise most of her young siblings to later run responsible families. That aunt never married. My mother was told she would never have children if she ever married. I was not to be born according to her doctor, for she would never have children. God had already decided otherwise…

In spite all the medical odds, I was born to both my parents when my mother was in her mid-thirties. They would recall my birth by telling the story of me as a newborn saying, "You winked at everyone when you were born." I came into the world winking one eye with a smile in declaration of how this child joyfully awaits the loving arms of the new proud humble parents.

Since my parents have been married in the Catholic church, it might have destroyed my own faith when they divorced due to my father's infidelities. However, it did not affect me too much since I was a sheltered child and felt loved by my family. Since they did not take me to church regularly or pray the rosary, how was I to understand the moral life of a Catholic?

But I believed in God, and I can still remember great spiritual moments from my childhood. When you read the spiritual dreams, you will understand!

Spiritual Moments of Seeing 'Love' in Others

For example, as a child, five years old, I remember seeing genuine love in the eyes of a teacher. It being the last day of school, the classroom had a Field Day with ice cream.

I spoke only Spanish. I had straight short hair with straight bangs across my forehead. I wore a simple yellow dress, probably a size four. I can still remember my teacher's eyes clearly, as she gently kneeled ground level to get direct eye contact with me since I was so small.

She held my hand while I held an ice cream cone in my other hand. I would not let go of the ice cream cone for the life of me! It did not matter to me or for that matter, even the teacher that my face was covered with ice cream. As she kissed my cheek tears came out of her eyes.

I looked into her eyes and saw in her genuine love and a deep fear, but a glimpse of hope for me. At this time, this small child stood still and quiet to analyze this teacher's face and attitude. I could feel her emotions and knew exactly what she was thinking as to how this small helpless child could learn to survive in this ever-changing world. Since it was the last day of school, it would be my last day with this caring teacher.

Even as a child, I by silently looking at the teacher, I felt these vibes flow back to me while holding my ice cream cone. It was a picture of a genuine loving and caring teacher, wishing the child a good life.

Looking at this caring teacher crying as she held my hand for the last time, I realized that there was a sign of fear for this young child's future in a crazy world. I could tell she was hoping for me to find my way into adult life without too many complications.

Even a small child can recognize genuine hope and love, even if only five years old. Small actions of love make a lifetime of difference.

The seed of faith planted by my parents continued to be nurturing me as I went onward in my journey of building faith.

Lesson on Life

Another time, when around six or seven years old, I was playing in the yard and saw a lifeless tiny, small bird laying on the concrete. I ran inside and asked my mother, "Please give me an empty matchbox."

My mother gave me an empty matchbox; I ran back outside with the matchbox. What did the small child do with the matchbox?

I placed the bird in the matchbox and called all my friends from the neighborhood. Basically, I told all my little neighborhood friends there would be a ceremony for the bird to give him a proper burial by praying for the bird.

We all knelt and prayed for the bird. This is a moment where prayer becomes a child's opportunity to influence her friends. There were sticks for candles, as the tiny bird was lying within its matchbox being marched around the house by these small children. We finally dug a small hole using a stick to dig and bury the matchbox in an earthen plot by my bedroom window.

A reflective moment now to wonder, as the other children grew up, it would be a marvel if they also got a slight glimpse of God in this childhood memory. As for me, it did…

So, how did this young child know instinctively to pray while playing with young children and to recognize the loss of life through the little bird? God is always instructing the young child by instinctively allowing it to recreate moments of compassion to be shared with their young friends. Children can be more sensitive than adults.

They can have an openness to the spiritual world while often the adult cannot understand. The moment might go unnoticed by the adult, but the child will always remember the moment.

Here is a spiritual incident when I was seven years old. I answered an urgent phone call at my home. It brought on panic and cries of horror for the adults. Upon answering the phone, I heard an awful wailing and a voice crying about a murder.

So, being a child, I simply yelled out and related the message to the family of the tragic news. The home was filled with wailing, yelling, screaming, and panicking as I made the loud announcement while still holding the receiver in my hand. What did the child do when tragedy struck entire families? I simply held the phone in my hand and silently watched them.

But there was one thing I did differently than all the adults. I made the sign of the cross multiple times, as I held the receiver in my other hand. I knew God was still in the midst of tragedy and sorrow, even as a young child among adults.

Now, how did I know to do this? I do not have an answer, but I realize now that even as a child I had recognized God, where the adults could not find Him in that particular moment. The adults were petrified by the shocking murder. I quickly blessed myself by making the sign of the cross while the adults grieved uncontrollably among themselves.

Perhaps, a child may have a different attitude towards pain and tragedy. The child sometimes with innocence discovers their pure message of faith without any murkiness to cloud its emotions.

A Gift for All Times

Finally, there was another strong spiritual moment I felt as a seven-year-old playing in a church courtyard with other children. I was attending religious classes in preparation for my First Communion on that day. However, there was time to go outside to play in the courtyard of the church.

While playing with the children, I noticed a lady whom I did not know nearby. She walks towards me and into the courtyard. I stop playing to turn around to acknowledge her presence as she entered the courtyard to speak to me.

The woman slightly bent over at the waist to reach my level and handed me a rosary. The lady only spoke to me out of all the children, as she gently grabbed my hand to place a wonderful scented purple olive rosary with a white cross into my hand.

I remember her telling me, "Here this will keep the devil away!" She clasped my hand with the rosary and turned around quickly and walk out of the courtyard.

The rosary had a beautiful scent and I kept it until I was an adolescent. It would hang on the rail of my bed until I was older. I did not know how to pray the rosary at this time.

So as simple a thing, as to giving a young child a rosary, may bring a significance impact while at the same time make a difference for his or her entire lifetime. This may happen even if it looks as if the child will not listen or know what one is saying to him or her. It will become the simple gift that gives faith and spiritual meaning throughout the lineage of generations to come. Something so small, a rosary becomes the greatest gift for the soul of a child and even in adulthood.

It is simply a grace to be gathered by a child for its future use. By praying around children, we show them the faith even if they look as if like they are not listening to us. They are listening with all their senses!

An Intuitive Moment

I remember being a young adult and having an awe moment or a moment where I suddenly comprehend and understood things in front of me. It may be difficult to explain or understand, so I will try my best to explain it.

It happened in the most unusual place, a carnival. I walked the grounds of the carnival looking at their games. I found a game booth which had a rotating multicolored spinning wheel, a quarter had to be placed on a color in hopes that the wheel would stop on the color.

If you get lucky, the constant rotating wheel will stop on the color you bet with a quarter hopefully on that winning color. Well, you need not guess any further because 'YOU

WIN!' The prize was a colorful fancy Victorian dressed up doll with its hat. So, this game caught my attention even if the odds of winning would be exceptionally low.

This was a moment for me, because I figured how to win all the time, I do mean each time! EVERYTIME!

Observation time first! I stood there watching how people were placing their quarters on the colors they thought would win them a prize.

Discovery time is next! The discovery of winning every game on my own after observing and silently watching people play the game was going to be an experience for the soul, soon.

As I looked around, I realized two things about the people around the game for they had not figured out: One, how to win every time! Two, the game may have been rigged by the carnival attender or operator of the game. Yes, this is real and true!

Figuring this out was done through patience and careful observation. Each new color where the dial landed was exactly, as for an example eight spaces from the previous one. This is what I call a moment of high intuition. Again, it was a moment where I had a high sense of intuition because I was able to determine what others around me did not bother to figure out.

Decision time! I pull out my first quarter to starting my winning streak. So here it goes my winning streak....

First, I placed my first quarter on a color. The game operator spins the wheel and it stops on the color my quarter was placed on.

So, great! I picked out my prize, a beautiful doll wearing a colorful fancy green Victorian dress.

Keep going onto the next round! I placed my second quarter on a color and watched as to where the spinning wheel will soon stop in this game.

The wheel stops and lands on the color where I placed my bet with the second quarter.

No need to guess! I won again, so I picked out the next prize, another colorful beautiful doll.

So, I did not stop playing the game! I continued the game by placing a quarter on a color on the rotating wheel I selected since it would be another definite win for me.

The wheel stopped on the color I had placed my bet on the wheel, AGAIN.

This winning streak continued for several games with the accumulation of several dolls, as winning prizes.

By now, the game attendant was feeling nervous, angry, and about to have a mental breakdown right there at his own tent area. I knew exactly what he was thinking, "How did this girl figure out how to win this game at every round?"

The game attendant's eye became night visions spotting a prey, for he did not dare to remove his eyes off me for a mere second as I slowly walked away from the winning streak game.

All of my senses felt his anger and I could intuitively hear him say, "Get out of here! Do not come back here!"

I just knew I had to leave before he got more upset. So, this is the moment I had decided to stop playing the game. So, I did just that, I walked away with my all my beautiful prizes.

Then an awe reflective moment came to me, as I walked away.

I saw a very worried man who was profiting from lying to the people; however, I brought his lies into the light by revealing it to him before himself and very publicly. He knew I had figured it out.

But, yet still a few failed to recognize the man's greed even if placed within their own reach; however, this young girl recognized it and it was so obvious that it became another teaching moment for the soul.

My rationale for walking away from the winning streak is "I am going to take all this man's profit if I stand here to play and clearly win every prize. Let me not be greedy. I'll walk away from here."

While walking away, I quickly turned around to get a glimpse of the man's eyes who was bewildered by a young girl who could easily bring his tent or house down.

Interestingly, this young girl's compassion became real, as I felt sorry for him because he was unable to fully recognize his true self since his facade concealed the good side of him.

You may ask, "How did you figure how to win every game all the time?"

Well, as I stood before the game in silence and before joining the game, I had a high sense of intuition. I cannot truly explain it, only to tell you, patience and observation were the key elements to help me during this moment of high intuition.

So, maybe now, I think it is beneficial for one to observe what we do carefully and have an abundance of patient so we can persevere in those critical moments within our own life.

What did I do during my observation of the game before joining to play the game, I stood back to patiently and carefully count the spaces in-between the first winning color and the next round's winning color, as people played their rounds of the game.

So, I finally figured the number of spaces between the first round and the next round of colors would always remain the same throughout the entire game, even if the colors would interchangeably be different in color at the winning rounds; For, the colors were prime colors on the multicolored rotating wheel, so you may have different winning alternative colors for a couple of rounds but the number would remain the same between the alternative colors. Usually people do not stick around to figure this out and move on after maybe winning one or two rounds in a game. Unless you figure it out like I did on this game.

When finally placing a quarter on the winning color, it would be the next color within the exact number of spaces from the previous winning color. Guess what? I won every single game every time!

So, as I went home for the evening it occurred to me, "How could no one else figure out what I figured out at the carnival? It is so simple." There was plenty of people around the wheel, yet no one figured it out.

So, I thought is there something wrong with me? This happened to be a high intuitive moment for me. However, the best thing is I was able to reflect on this moment, and I realized it was a moment of high intuition with a teaching lesson on greed for the soul.

How did I turn it into a teaching moral moment? I could have been greedy just like the game operator, but I chose to make a wise choice of simply walking away. I just let the man make his living and at the same time allowed him to take a quick reflective moment in his soul as he stood in utter silence wishing for me to leave the premises; for his profits were at risk. He had a glimpse of how his soul was brought into a glimpse of light reflecting on his mind and soul, for this a moment for him to always remember and reflect during his life.

So, the gift is not that I won all the time. The gift is knowing as a young adult, what was morally wrong, though the adult, a carnival attendant or game operator did not know it was morally wrong to mislead his game players. That is the gift or the real prize! It is the ability to recognize what is morally wrong in any moment of time for a young adult!

I realize God was using this moment to teach me about morality, though in the secular world, sometimes morality cannot be found. MORALITY shows up and keeps us from greedy moments caused by the actions of other souls.

As children grow up into the adolescent stage, they lose their childish traits, but they build their character based on their childhood experiences. This is not saying a child, who may have a terrible childhood, cannot experience the spiritual realm. However usually children have experiences relating to life differently than adults. A wonderful experience for a young teenager may give them a road map into their adulthood. It did for me!

Education

As an adult, already a wife and a mother I graduated from Texas A&M-Corpus Christi University with a bachelor degree in English. My mother had passed away years before I graduated from college. Since I knew my dad's health was slowly declining, I made it a goal to make sure to get a higher education degree so my dad could witness a dream of his, my college graduation. If I could give that day a name rather than my college graduation day, it would be 'Dad's Day' because he smiled more brightly than the graduate.

Married Life

Let us now talk about my marriage. I found marriage to be my vocation after ten years of dating my first husband! Yes, it was eight years of dating and two years of engagement! Everyone was thrilled when we decided to set a time for the wedding. The one word we heard was "finally" over and over again.

The decision to have a long engagement was made by me, since I told my husband, "I will not move out of my parent's home to move into an apartment. We must make every effort to purchase a house before the marriage." In other words, I did not see the logic in moving from a home into an apartment.

The marriage did not take place until we purchased our first home. The engagement period gave us time to buy and pay off all the new furniture before the marriage. Meanwhile, until the marriage took place, the new furniture would crowd the hallways and rooms of my mother's house. It became impossible to walk!

We continued buying furniture to fill our home and stored it within my mother's home. We did not move the new furniture into our new purchased home since we did not live in the home. Since we did not live in the new home, we feared vandalism in the vacant home.

I will never forget my family's reaction of happiness a week before my wedding when I told them the furniture would be moved out their home into our new home. It was one of the happiest moments of their life!

It was a gratitude of "Thank God, now we can walk freely in our own hallways and rooms."

Now about our new cute home, I lovely called it, 'Our

Little Grandma Home,' because it was an antique style home with real hardwood flooring throughout the entire house. The interior of the home is beautiful! It would be vacant until we moved into the home on our wedding day, October 09, 1993.

The Cathedral High Mass wedding with the entire mass sung by the priest and a full singing Cathedral Pontifical Choir, made a proud dad boldly say, "There will never be another wedding like this in the family."

He was right, so far, I have not seen a Cathedral High Mass wedding with a full Pontifical Choir in the family, but I hope to see another one with joy. It would bring good memories back to me.

Humorously I thought: One good thing about not being a Cathedral bride is she probably will not have a migraine headache from wearing a heavy headpiece and walking a long aisle with a twenty-two-foot Cathedral dress train known as the Monarch Style on her wedding day as I did in 1993. Whew! I was tired!

In December of 1995, I gave birth to full-term healthy twin girls. All doctor visits recorded normal blood pressure with zero swelling to any of my extremities throughout the entire pregnancy of the twins, also I continued working until my maternity leave within a hospital. Throughout my pregnancy, I did not suffer from any morning sickness. So, it was a good and an excellent pregnancy of delivery of twins.

However, it was not the case for my husband during that time. He had consistent swelling of his feet to the point of being unable to tie his shoes. He had escalating high blood pressure. Yes, there was a silent foe, and it was yet to be discovered within the marriage.

How was this young Catholic family going to fight against

this foe in their marriage? What was the foe in the marriage? The marriage luring foe would not be discovered until my husband's kidney biopsy.

The kidney biopsy revealed the evil invader of the marriage, Lupus Nephritis. It would within a couple of years claim the life of my husband for Lupus may be a difficult disease.

Lupus places many restrictions on a person due to fatigue, increasingly abnormal high blood pressure and medications, it is difficult when lupus invades the organs such as the kidneys.

We made a decision, and it was an easy one for me. I decided to work until the end of my pregnancy, since I had the best medical insurance from working in a hospital. I would keep the job until my maternity leave to deliver twin full term babies.

I worked right until it was close to my delivery at a hospital trauma center within its emergency room since my husband could no longer work due to illness. My work week would be as follow: two eight hour shifts back-to-back on Friday, and the same on Saturday ending with an eight-hour shift on Sunday. In other words, I would do all forty hours within the three days and be off work for the next four days.

You may think she must have been exhausted and tired of working! At first, it was normal routine but after some time it became totally exhausting to later in life to think about the slight idea of working. Call it 'burned-out!'

I must confess the sole reason in keeping my job was the excellent health benefits for our entire family. If I remember correctly, the cost of my hospital delivery of twins was under one hundred dollars under my medical plan. Financially, it was important to keep this medical coverage for the two newborns and our family. The medical insurance would now help my husband with his medical cost of Lupus Nephritis, for we never received any kind of assistance from the state or at all. Never! This is the financial part of my first marriage, but spiritual guidance would soon put more life into our bodies and souls, even making the harsh times seem like a breeze in life.

The Quiet One

In our marriage, we heavily leaned on was the Church for spiritual direction. This gave us peace within our lovely home! Spiritual direction was a necessity for us.

My husband was blessed to have a spiritual director in 1996-98, a priest Father Manuel Hernandez (aka Fr. Meme), Rector of St. Patrick's Church and later also Rector of Our Lady of Guadalupe in Corpus Christi. He gifted my husband with the full authority of the church, a 'Full Plenary Indulgence' in 1996 or 1997, for naming one of the twins, Theresa Marie in Spanish the name is Teresa Maria.

Approximately, a year later, after receiving the plenary indulgence, my husband died on January 22, 1998, at the age of thirty-three years old. The twin daughters had just turn two years old a month earlier. Fr. Meme was a great blessing to our little Catholic family. God bless our priest! We have wonderful priest among us!

Yes, the church has its rituals and sacraments. They are extraordinary and very real. All we must do is reach out to the church for their blessings to obtain the sacraments, graces, and gifts of the Church.

Just as one of the graces from the church is to have a priest bestow a plenary indulgence, it may be partial or a full plenary indulgence just as the one gifted to my husband. It is a beautiful grace and gift. A wonderful gift by the church!

It was important for us to reach out to the Church because we had many spiritual happenings in our marriage and the Church was ready to help us in nurturing our souls to bring us close to God's love. As mentioned, one of the graces from the Church is to have a priest bestow a plenary indulgence to the penitent. It is a grace and a gift.

An indulgence, whether partial or plenary are gifts by the church. An indulgence may be applied to either to oneself or to the souls of the deceased and it will not apply to another person living on earth. Basically, a plenary indulgence is a full remission of temporal punishment from a sin (Cannon law 993).

In summary, a person cannot give any indulgences gifted by the Church to a friend down the street. It does not work that way!

So, why was my husband gifted a plenary indulgence by Fr. Meme for naming one of the twins, Theresa Maria (aka Teresa Maria)? I will explain the significance of her name.

First, I never had a normal spiritual life. This spiritual encounter one night would be kept a family secret with a few people knowing about the encounter, which would include my husband's spiritual director. What I will relate to you is true and a known fact in my life but kept silent for it may not be seen by many as real or just too unrealistic. However, as for me, it is realistic, true and continues to be true without being prideful I make this statement.

I was several months pregnant with twin girls. My first husband excitedly woke me up, "Wake up! Wake up! The Blessed Mother Mary was here, and the room smells like roses, wake up! It smells like roses in here!" I woke up to see him looking ecstatically happy.

He proceeds to tell me, "She stood in front of the bed."

33

He ecstatically continues to tell me, "Mary spoke in Spanish." Sitting up in bed I asked him, "What in Spanish?" and "What did Mary tell you?" He replied, "In Spanish she told me, No te mortifiques que tu papa estara bien, pero de las dos la mas calladitas le llamaras Teresa Maria."

I will now translate for you, "Do not worry yourself for your father shall be fine; But of the two, the quiet one name her Teresa Maria." My husband continued by telling me, "Hurry, let's get up and pray the rosary to Mary."

We prayed the three mysteries of the rosary, and the naming of the child remained a family secret. His parents would lovingly bring it up once and awhile when they would see my daughter and call her lovingly, 'The Quiet One.'

Just as my husband stated his father's health issues were completely restored, as revealed to my husband by Mary. Later in life, his father developed other health issues such as forgetting about his surroundings, yet it was certainty that he was a proud father and grandfather.

However, this would not be my only encounter with Mary, Most Holy for I would soon have an encounter prior to my second marriage.

One thing I am proud to mention is that my first husband, Rodolfo, left this world knowing the twins would be raised Catholic. I promised my husband while he was dying that the twins would grow up not only in name Catholic but would become practicing Catholics. I told him not to worry about this because I would make sure they would become practicing Catholics.

The baptized Catholic twins grew up and continued the religion of myself and their father by serving God in the Catholic church since the age seven through adulthood. So, my children are now adults.

I will testify all three of my children have become excellent Catholics. My son is a Lector for the Cathedral in Corpus Christi and one of my daughters teaches religion classes in a local parish, while my other daughter reads spiritual books. They all attend Catholic Masses on Sundays and holy days of obligation. The most important thing is I do not have to tell them to go to Sunday Mass for they automatically drive themselves to Mass on their own without us parents telling them. That makes us indeed proud parents!

The twins, Kristian Faith and Theresa Marie grew up beautifully and hold several college degrees and continue working on their furthering their college education after two associate degrees from a community college, one in chemistry and another in biology. They also have a bachelor's degrees in biology with a concentration in microbiology from a university. Currently, they are working on Nursing degrees.

My son, Douglas H. Harley holds one college degree from a local community college in Art and is currently a straight "A" University student. He is still in the pursuit of a higher education at a university while illustrating the artwork within this book.

So, how did I manage to keep all three of my adult children happy in our home even as adult children? Simple answer! God! 'The more you pursue Him the more you will catch Him,' this also goes for one's homelife and families. God must be at the center of everything since the moment the children are born even if it may be exhausting to wake them up early on Sunday's, as they fuss about being woken up to attend Mass, it is something that must be done. Rain, shine, wind, or snow for it must be done!

Why? They will learn about God and acquire graces as they age even if unseen at the time.

Before, I proceed to tell you how or share with you on how I kept the faith during times of sorrow or mourning I will tell you an experience while awake before my husband's death. The reason in mentioning this to you because it is a moment experienced while awake and not sleeping.

The Night of Horror

This is an actual experience of a night where I was unable to fall asleep. There seem to be an uneasy feeling and there-fore, I just laid in bed without falling asleep. It is like the body senses trouble.

This is the horrifying experience that I remember until this day and will never forget.

The bedroom was completely dark for it was time to go to sleep yet I was unable to sleep this night. Suddenly, I felt a strong presence at my bedroom door, so I sat up in my bed. With my own two eyes, I saw an evil dark shadow at my bedroom door.

The room was completely dark, but I could see this shadow slowly walking into my bedroom. The tall dark shadow completely draped in black walks into my bedroom.

Now, it slowly turns around to face me! It looks straight at me. It was totally draped in black from its head to toe with green eyes. The color of the eyes could be compared to the green traffic signal lights at night.

I could see no face but only its eyes. This thing was dark-er than the dark room itself, so I could see dark within the dark. My husband was asleep, and I was too scared to wake him up. As I sat up looking at this dark thing, I said out loud, "Oh, my God!"

What happen next? The dark shadow with its green eyes and no face suddenly does something unusual, it puts it head down or bows its head in front of me to slowly turn back around to walk away from where it came from to exit the bedroom door. After, I mentioned God, it made a decision to not want to look at me and to exit the bedroom. It took one hard look at me and put its head down and turns backs around to exit through the bedroom door. Also, I did have the Sacred Heart of Jesus image over my bed where I slept and up to this day I still have it over my bed. It has been close to three decades since this happen but I can remember every detail of that night.

It was a terrifying night for me! My husband's death would take place several months after this, so this may have been a foreshadowing moment of death.

After discussing this with my husband, we decided to have a priest with a couple of invited guest come over for a Mass in our home.

We would be having an 'Enthronement to the Sacred Heart of Jesus and the Immaculate Heart of Mary' in our small home. The enthronement would be placed in the Living Room area of the home, where it is also the main entrance to the home. I still have the enthronement from this home. Just beautiful enthronements!

There is a solution to everything: Faith. The solution to fear is to bring more faith to those around us. Some may say, 'I have faith' but listen what was told by Jesus, "For amen I say to you, if you have faith the size of a mustard seed, you will say to this mountain, 'Move from here to there,' and it will move. Nothing will be impossible to you." (Matthew 17:20). Jesus's words resonated in the heart; therefore, this strong faith remained with us and continued to build around our small Catholic family even in those dark moments. Soon others would partake in this strong faith without realizing it!

Faith moves all barriers and mountains!

Also, note when Jesus spoke, he was speaking directly to the soul of a person. The soul lies within the heart of a man. How does one get strong faith? Sometimes we find faith in dark moments like in mourning or sorrow. In surrendering all to God, the cross gets lighter for if we refuse to carry crosses in suffering then the cross gets heavier and heavier. I realized then I must forget about myself and focus on a strong faith and share it.

Stronger Faith is all We Need

How did I focus on a stronger faith and help people in the midst of my own sorrow? My husband's funeral and the father of the two-year-old twins gave me an opportunity to bring faith to all. It first started out with all present at the funeral witnessing the faith of my husband, who was a practicing Catholic with lots of faith.

An excellent retired priest, Fr. Pete McNamara upon learning about my husband's death, he decided to be the celebrant for the Mass and drove himself from Zapata, Texas to Corpus Christi, Texas. The priest told the crowd of people, "I remember Rodolfo (my husband) during his youth was under my direction, as an altar server. He always had shiny shoes for Mass." Everyone loved the comment from Fr. McNamara, for it was the simple truth!

It was a difficult three days! The third day after the funeral, when I closed my eyes to relax, all I could see as I laid in my bed was the shaking of peoples' hands non-stop, repeatedly throughout the entire three days. It felt that way! The amount of people was huge, and it was a standing room only within the church.

This was a sorrowful time, but also I saw this time as an opportunity to build up faith to those around me. My promise to my husband was to raise the two-year-old twin children as good Catholics and starting at that moment faith would grow even stronger. It would be the best gift I could extend to them during this sorrowful moment, as they would be able to witness when they grew up by watching videos and pictures of their father's funeral. I hire a professional photographer and videographer to have the funeral filmed for the young twins' collection of their father life.

Well, this became an opportunity to set souls on fire, so I started here for it was as if I was transported out of my own body into a new body with the mission to shed light to others around me. It was a mission! I had to forget about my own grieving and sorrow and put others first, such as my children and other mourners. I knew this would be the time!

It became important to me on stressing to others how God is with us even through times of losing a loved one such as a parent and a husband. I decided not to dwell on myself, but to think about all those people who lost faith or live with a diminished faith or even question their own faith because prayers would go unanswered due to illness or a loss of a family or friend. I decide this is the time to bring faith to all and be brave without crying at all during my eulogy.

So, before the funeral, I personally wrote the eulogy from the heart to address the crowd of people after the rosary by speaking the following:

> First of all, I would like to thank God for my husband, who never feared death, but viewed death as an embrace in Jesus' arms. My husband had a strong Catholic faith, which will also be passed on to his children, Kristian Faith, and Theresa Marie. Perhaps this suffering of losing my husband could diminish my faith, but, on

the contrary, my faith in God and the Church is greater. I accept God's will and will not fight against it but will only continue to pray for my children to grow up not part Catholic, but as devoted Catholics, just as planned throughout our marriage. I would like to thank everyone, who supported our family through prayers and love during this time of sorrow. God bless each one of you and your families. (Eulogy 1998)

After my first husband passed away, I quit my job to remain at home with the children. Financially, the twins and I were doing well in our home so I could stay at home with them. I would now seek a ministry at my own will and choice as I contacted a hospital to become a Eucharistic Minister in 1998 to the sick. I will explain how I decided to become a Eucharistic Minister at a hospital.

An Encounter with Our Blessed Mother

This ministry came about after my encounter with Our Blessed Mother. My new ministry was to take the Eucharist to patients throughout the hospital. This ministry was under the direction of Fr. Kizito, an excellent priest to all who meet him! I along with the owner of a highly publicized moving concrete statue of the Blessed Mother, Mary that would move, cry, walk out of the niche and turn her head here within the City of Corpus Christi, Texas by Moody High School, well, would now become Eucharistic Ministers to the sick.

We went together to distribute the Eucharist to patients in the hospital. We practically went to every single floor except for the isolation rooms to distribute the eucharist. It was beautiful.

In remembering the beauty of praying the rosary, the two-year-old twins and I would visit the moving statue and pray with all the massive amount of people around the home where the statue was located in Corpus Christi, Texas. The media was very intense around the statue that evening and soon the news media show, '48 Hours' would be coming to Corpus Christi to visit the statue; however, it did not happen. When it came to praying the rosary, I would lead the rosary at times on microphone and learned to also pray in Spanish, as taught by the ladies at the rosary. I would pray for the sick and those requesting prayer, but I would also pray for the intentions of a good husband and wished to become a mother once again by having another child.

It is through the intercession of Our Blessed Mother the prayers were answered for within months she sent me a husband. He would soon be arriving from a pilgrimage in Medjugorje and would soon be an excellent father to my twin daughters, for he had no children of his own and never had married in his lifetime. Yes, God answered my prayers through the intercession of his Holy Mother, Mary. It was almost as if I had written a prescription to God and HE filled it exactly as through the intercession of Our Blessed Mother Mary, Most Holy.

Soon the gift of life was given to us through this bundle of joy, our beautiful baby boy, Douglas Harley born on December 08.

Later, Seventeen-days old, Douglas would be laying in a manger in front of the Church altar throughout the Christmas Midnight Mass, as a Baby Jesus. The church was not the church we usually attended on Sundays but an organization at this church knew I had a baby boy, so they called to ask if we would help them out. We were honored to participate at the Christmas Mass.   We were so proud of our little son; for, he did not cry at all and enjoyed sleeping in the manger up in front of the altar for over an hour and a half. This Christmas night was a true gift of peace and happiness for all present!

I believe through the power of intercession of Our Blessed Mother, Mary, God listened to all the prayers.

Regarding meeting my husband, Doug, I would say God picked a particular day to bring us together since we had not met yet, since we were in two opposite parts of the world. Each of one of us being a part of a Marian apparitions within the same time. The day we met would be the Feast of the Sacred Heart. Two years later we would be married in a Catholic Church on the same feast day we met, *The Feast of the Sacred Heart.*

Marian Experience

I will tell you about Doug's Marian experience since I already told you about my Marian experience.

Prior to Doug and I meeting, he had just returned from Medjugorje several months before we met in Corpus Christi.

While in Medjugorje he stayed within the home of the visionary, Mirjana Soldo for a week or nine days. This is where he had a personal encounter of Our Blessed Mother, as the visionary was having her vision in her home basement one day.

Doug was now present in the Marian encounter, for the Visionary, Mirjana Soldo's was having a vision and visitation within her own home of Our Blessed Mother, Mary.

A wonderful experience Doug and I enjoy talking about is his visit to Medjugorje in 1998. Doug talks about his experience at Mirjana Soldo's home. He said, "I knelt and prayed with all of my heart." And he continues to say that he told the Blessed Mother while she was appearing, "Mary come into my heart" during the apparition in the home of the visionary, Mirjana Soldo.

What happens next is amazing! My husband, Doug states his entire chest started to burn and did not stop burning until the Blessed Mother Mary ceased appearing to the visionary. He had been staying in the home for a couple of days when he encountered Our Blessed Mother Mary.

We have actual video of Doug in the home of Mirjana and directly asking her questions. Upon his return to Corpus Christi, we met during the Feast of the Sacred Heart at a local parish's adoration night. A couple of years later, Doug would kneel down in the Cathedral Adoration Chapel, as I prayed, as he suddenly held a beautiful diamond ring in his hand and proposed the question, "Will you marry me?" So, you know the answer to that question, now!

God choose a Feast Day for my husband and I to meet, and in adoring God through perpetual adoration, we found the sacrament of marriage and the unification of a family in a beautiful city known as the 'City by the Bay.'

My second Catholic marriage took place at the Corpus Christi Cathedral on the Feast of the Sacred Heart, which was also the celebration of the Feast Day of the Sacred Heart of Jesus, for it was the day we met for the first time and would now marry on this beautiful Feast Day of the Sacred Heart of Jesus. So, yes, I have been married twice in the local Cathedral of Corpus Christi, Texas.

When I made my petitions to Our Blessed Mother, Mary in prayer, I was very specific about a person I wished for in my future life. Mary always does things perfectly, as she petitioned God for me, as I expressed to her that I wished for someone to be single, with no responsibilities and intelligent and in petitioning I went on and on and on...

Well, Doug Harley, a handsome single man had never been married or did not have any children for he had recently retired from the military. He retired as a Navy Officer a couple of years before we met at the age of thirty-five years old without any disabilities.

At that time, the Navy was offering early retirement for anyone who wished to retire early after serving so many years of service, in his case, he received credit for sixteen and half years of service. The monthly retirement and medical benefits for life, which were immediate upon his retirement would now include his new family, which gave our new family financial freedom.

Doug was grateful to serve the military since they provided him many training opportunities and educational opportunities. Upon graduating with all honors from the University of Texas and traveling all the 'Seven Seas' in a submarine and throughout the world; there was no other place more perfect than the beautiful 'City by the Bay,' officially named, Corpus Christi, Texas to retire and settle down to start a family.

Even after living in Hawaii for two years, the most alluring place to settle down to raise a family would be Corpus Christi, Texas. I can only image that a life in a submarine is not a life for everyone but what I can say for certainty is, "What a way to travel!"

Doug was a convert into the Catholic faith. After retiring from the military, he discovered the Catholic church in 1995 and fell in love with all of it. He became an excellent practicing Catholic, helping in ministries such as Eucharistic Minister and filling in on hours of Eucharistic Perpetual Adoration.

My husband, Doug is now a College Math Professor and

an excellent father to three adult children: Kristian Faith and Theresa Marie Lopez, Douglas H. Harley. Our son, Douglas sketched the dreams (visions) in the book. He is a talented young man!

Now, I wish to proceed to tell you about a Eucharistic Miracle.

Eucharistic Miracle
in the Diocese of Corpus Christi, Texas

Now, that you are familiar with the family I want to tell you about a miracle during Holy Week of 2018. A Eucharistic miracle!

Yes, this is what I call it for it happened during Holy Week of 2018.

Again, I will let you know I interpret this to be a Eucharistic miracle!

It happened at the Corpus Christi Cathedral in Texas on Holy Thursday, March 29, 2018. I will explain it to you.

Our family attends the Triduum, which is the 'Three Holy Days' of Holy Week. It starts on Holy Thursday, Good Friday and Holy Saturday known as Easter Vigil. Our children were Altar Servers at the mass on the first day of the Triduum, which is Holy Thursday; therefore, it was my husband and I sitting at one of the pews in church.

Suddenly, Doug tells me during holy communion with his eyes closed, "Call an ambulance! I feel terrible!" I could not believe what I was hearing at the time! He is not one to complain about being sick.

However, my strong faith did not banish from me but unexplainably became even stronger and stronger within me. What I did next was based on having a super strong faith and seeing God in everything even during this awful moment.

I told him, "Yes, but I am bringing Bishop Mulvey back with me to give you communion before we leave." So, I walked towards Bishop Mulvey, who was dispensing the Eucharist in front of the church.

As I approached the Bishop of the Diocese of Corpus Christi I asked him, "Bishop, my husband Doug has a severe headache. Can you please give him communion?

The kind bishop without hesitating immediately walked with the chalice to find my husband sitting down and shaking from pain at the pew.

Bishop Mulvey distributed the 'Body of Christ' to my husband Doug sitting within the church pew. My husband Doug was in severe pain and could not take the Eucharist in his mouth, therefore, he took the Eucharist in his hand to only put his entire mouth onto his own hand to eat the Eucharist.

He was shaking so much he had no control of his fingers, so he had to place his mouth on his own palm of his hand to eat the Eucharist. I believe this is where the miracle took place upon eating the Eucharist. I will come back to this thought. An ambulance arrived and he was placed on a gurney inside the Cathedral. I gave my keys to someone at the church to give to one of my children who at the time was serving in church to drive themselves to the hospital after the Holy Thursday Mass.

As I walked away and stood at the double doors of the church and looking before me was the beautiful golden tabernacle a short distance away I said to HIM, "May your will be done! In Jesus name, whose name is above all names." I proceeded to genuflect, while I made the sign of the cross in strong faith and proceeded to walk out with my husband

46

into the ambulance. The ambulance took us down the street, a five-minute distance to the hospital since the church is within walking distance, as to where our family home is over twenty minutes away from the hospital. The whole night was a miracle, as you read further on you will understand.

Later, my husband would recall and felt sorrowful about his last recollection or memory of not having voluntary motor skills to take communion in the mouth due to the shaking and intense pain in his brain. So, he had to eat the Eucharist from the palm of his hand. He told me later that his fingers would not work because of too much shaking so the only thing he could do is eat the Eucharist from his palm. It was a sorrowful moment.

He does remembers opening his eyes to look at the eucharist before eating it out of his palm. This is the last thing he remembered from this night! As soon as he ate the Eucharist, Jesus took the pain and the memory of pain from THAT moment on until his surgery.

At the Cathedral when the ambulance arrived, my husband was given a plastic bag to throw up, as he threw up blood in this bag. I rode with him in the ambulance down the street about five minutes from the church. Doug was praying the rosary in the ER room and answered all questions correctly when asked by medical personal. He did not agonize at all about pain yet was in pain while in the ER.

He had a CT scan of the brain, and the diagnosis came back as a brain bleed. They told us the brain shifted nine millimeters. If the brain would have shifted to ten millimeters, he would have gone into a coma and not come out of it.

This is where the miracle took place! The miracle started when my husband Doug consumed, 'Jesus in the Eucharist,' the brain shift stopped at that time. The brain

stopped shifting for it was shy one millimeter from the stage of being comatose. This is the miracle! Jesus took over the pain by numbing him and stopping the brain from shifting by that fragile one millimeter. Yes, one millimeter.

Upon taking the Eucharist, Jesus took over the intense suffering and the pain stopped even though Doug was unaware, he was effectively communicating and praying the full decades of the rosary out loud while in the emergency room. However, he does not remember praying or communicating with others or anything after consuming the Eucharist at the Cathedral on Holy Thursday.

In fact, he does not remember anything after taking holy communion or the intensity of the pain. Jesus took care of the pain and numbed it! But wait, there were even more surprises…

In the emergency room, I asked the medical staff, "Who is Neurosurgeon? Can I speak to the Neurosurgeon?" I was told the name of the doctor. I was surprised beyond belief upon hearing the name of the surgeon that would be operating my husband's brain.

Shocked! Upon hearing the name of the doctor, I could not believe it!

The reason for this shock is because on March 20, 2018 I had taken a relative of mine to see this particular Neurosurgeon for my relative neurological problem. While in this doctor's office with my relative: the neurosurgeon, relative and myself had a lengthy conversation with the doctor. We left the office after her consultation with this doctor. My relative problem was unresolved due to other complications.

Well, now it is two weeks later on March 29, 2018, I am in the Emergency Room with my husband speaking to this precise doctor, who would be operating not on a relative but on my husband. So, I asked again, "Can I speak to the doctor?" They told me, "No! They will be gathering up a team tomorrow morning."

So, I made an instinctive call to the Neurosurgeon's answering service. God made sure that the answering service put me through to the doctor. Yes, I got to the doctor on the phone. I was now talking to the neurosurgeon on the phone.

I asked the Neurosurgeon, "Do you remember me? I was in your office with a relative?"

I explained about my relative to the doctor. The Neurosurgeon answered me, "Yes, I remember you."

Then I said, "Well, it is not my relative but my husband you will be operating soon for he has a brain bleed." I continued to tell the doctor, "We are now in the emergency room waiting for him to be seen by you."

The doctor said, "I will get my surgical team together in the morning." Just as the staff had mentioned to me. So, I cried about this scary moment but mostly I prayed about it.

The next day, the kind Bishop Mulvey prayed for my husband, Doug at the Holy Friday Services at Noon and at the very same time Doug would be on the operating table having brain surgery. Yes, on Good Friday Doug was having brain surgery exactly at Noon.

He would be having surgery right as the church service would take place at noon on Good Friday. So, God had his finger on everything!

After surgery, Doug went to ICU for several days and finally returned to our home. He would be fine until several months later.

A second brain bleed occurred on January 06, 2019. The new CT scan showed new blood being on top of the old blood causing high pressure on the brain. This was causing some numbness to left side of his body.

A second brain surgery would now take place on the opposite side of his brain to relieve the pressure and swelling in the brain. Again, God answered our prayers for the same neurosurgeon stops the bleeding and swelling by cauterizing it. Thank God!

As I write this in 2022, all new CT scans of the brain show resolved with zero abnormalities and no deficiencies. Doug does not take any medications and has no deficiencies up to now. On occasions, there may be migraine headaches and may have it checked out through the emergency room. The only medication Doug has is pain meds only if as needed for a migraine headache. The emergency room CT scans have shown the brain to be normal up to this date.

After two brain surgeries, any migraine headaches are expected and considered normal in most situations. He keeps active as he resumed working as a college math professor. He does all his normal routines of exercising, reading, daily Mass and family activities. We are grateful to God and thank Him! The Neurosurgeon even mentioned to me, "I will never forget this case."

This is where a Saint Blesses and Visits

A popular saint visits me! Now listen to this! While my husband's suffered a second brain bleed and is in the hospital this is where I had a saint visit me in a dream after praying the rosary and falling to sleep even though I never prayed to the saint. He is a popular saint, so I did know who he was when he presented or revealed himself to me in my dream.

Doug had swelling and incredibly low blood pressure; therefore, he was being monitored closely by the ICU staff after his second brain surgery.

Well, a saint I do not pray to revealed himself to me in a dream. The saint is Padre Pio, it is a dream written in Chapter Eighteen in this book. Just in case you would like to refer to the dream.

Now, praying the rosary is a great part of our daily lives. Eventually, the rosary, when prayed by a family, will give the petitioners many graces. They may not always be able to view the graces at the precise moment of their prayer, but it will slowly be revealed to them as time goes on… 'God does things in small steps not all at once.' It is the way He works in everyone's life.

The Graces of Praying the Rosary

I will give you another example of obtaining a grace by devoutly praying the rosary. This is a story about two young men who decided to walk a couple of blocks down the street for a night of fun at a local bar. It was a night of carousing with an entertaining evening for both the young men.

One of the two young men said, "I've had enough! I am going home to sleep. I will talk to you in the morning." His friend replied, "I'm staying here. I'll see you in the morning." The first young man walked away drunk down the street. He passes a local church. He is well acquainted with the priest at the church.

He passes the church and finally unlocks the door to his apartment. The young man goes upstairs to lay down in his bed but finds himself tossing around. Unable to fall asleep, for now he remembers something he does devoutly every night, "I forgot to pray the rosary. Maybe this why I cannot fall asleep."

He was accustomed to praying the rosary nightly before falling asleep. After praying the rosary, he fell asleep without any problems. Now, it is dawn.

Someone is banging loudly on his door. It is a non-stop loud banging on his door.

The young man, thinking it is his drunk friend, says, "Why is he knocking on my door so hard, if he has a key?" He goes down the stairs and opens the door.

He is astonished and scared at what he sees at the door. It was not human but a demon. The demon tells him, "Were you expecting your friend? Do not expect him because his soul is no longer here. We have it in HELL!" and continues to tell him, "If you want proof to this, go walk down the middle of the street and you will find your friend's burned up clothing in the center of the street."

The demon disappeared and the young man ran down the street to find his friend. He was horrified to find his friend's clothing and shoes smoldering with no body in sight.

So, he ran to get the priest he knew from the church. They both returned to look at the smoldering items in the center of the street.

Later, in discussion with the priest, the young man realizes how he survived the demonic night and why his friend was taken straight to hell by the demons.

The priest tells him, "You had a grace stored up for a night like this and sometimes we cannot see the immediate results of praying the rosary. You have now seen the results of praying the rosary. This is reason you could not sleep that night until you prayed your rosary. Our Blessed Mother Mary protected you and came to your aide, as you rely on and pray to her every night through the power of the rosary, as it is protection from evil. Evil could not touch you but avoided you because of your strong devotion to the holy rosary."

The priest continued, "Your friend never prayed the rosary. This is the reason the demons could so easily take over his life and take him to Hell on that night. You need not to pray for your friend, since you no longer can pray for someone that is in hell. Continue praying for yourself and others!" So, pray the rosary to acquire graces throughout one's life.

The spiritual realm involves teaching moments (awake or asleep), live moments (while awake) and dreaming moments (while asleep). I have been through all three cycles of these spiritual realm. A priest told me these are not dreams but interior visions, however, I will call them dreams. Actually, I have consulted with a Master Spiritual Director and in Pastoral Ministry, several priest including an exorcist and of course, my friend, who thought my dreams are not dreams but 'Interior Visions.'

I would like to mention, Dr. Ronda Chervin, my good friend and mentor. She encouraged me on a daily basis to be a confident writer by expressing the truths of the spiritual realm or world that I have in dreams but known as Interior Visions.

Dr. Chervin is known best for being the best as: An International Speaker, Philosopher, Professor of Theology and Philosophy (Doctor of Spirituality), a Visionary, a brilliant Writer of over sixty books and most of all a great Catholic and has taught many priest over the decades in Seminaries and Universities.

She gave me every reason to listen to her mentoring me daily at my home as I write about my dreams or Interior Visions. We would even take walks or drive around town just to talk about God and the visions.

An interesting fact, Dr. Chervin had excellent mentors, her own Godparents, Dietrich Von Hildebrand called 'the twentieth-century Doctor of the Church' by Pope Pius XII.

53

Dietrich Von Hildebrand married a great famous Catholic philosopher, Alice Von Hildebrand. So, I thank God for the gifts of my wonderful mentor and brilliant Catholic friend, Dr. Ronda Chervin and assisting me with my gifts. Dr. Chervin, as I always tell you, "You are the Best!" So, when I asked God for help this is what he gave me and I am so grateful.

It is now time to share the dreams with you. Let us travel together in a Spiritual Journey to Eternity based on my dreams known as 'Interior Visions.'

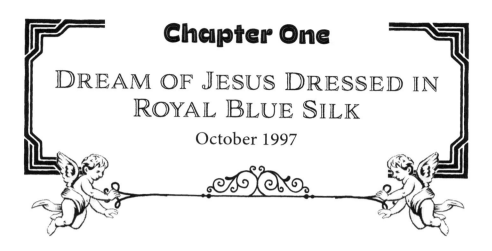

Chapter One

DREAM OF JESUS DRESSED IN ROYAL BLUE SILK

October 1997

*T*he dream takes place within a church, where I am standing in the center aisle looking at someone praying intensely, as this person is kneeling in a pew close to the church altar. This young man is praying with great faith in a serene manner. The young man with nicely trimmed dark hair wears a white mid-sleeve shirt with vertical blue strips on it. Intensely, he is praying on the front pew's kneeler. I could only see his back at a distance as he prayed and I closely watched the young man pray with intensity.

The important part of this dream is the young man is not alone as he prays in the church. In front of him was a man that he did not notice, the man was unnoticeable to the praying young man.

Yet, the man could hear the intense prayers of this young man kneeling before Him. Yes, it was Jesus Christ dressed in a silk garment of the deepest royal blue with the color of His eyes matching the silk garment as He listens to the praying man. Jesus stood in front of this young man, yet the young man who prayed with intensity could not visibly see Jesus watching him pray with all of his heart.

However, I stood at a slight distance in the aisle of the church viewing the most beautiful color of the deepest royal blue and the silk of the garment in which the silk resembles water. This silk garment was worn by Our Lord, Jesus Christ as He stood in front of the praying man. The deep royal blue garment of extreme silky material may be compatible to deep blue water. The silk could be closely described so smooth as to the flow of water. Upon looking at Jesus dressed in deep royal blue before the young man things soon changed and became intense, as my eyes gazed into His eyes from a short distance. In other words, Jesus now fixed his eyesight on me, as I stood at a distance and returning the look with the inability to take my eyes off Him. For it became impossible to remove my eyes from looking directly at His eyes even for a mere second, as He stood beautifully draped in royal blue silk attire that matched the color of His own eyes.

Now, I will describe Jesus as I saw him in this dream.

Jesus's stature was of slender build, and I describe Him to be tall for he was not short, as I viewed him at a slight distance. His complexion was very clear. The royal blue silk garment draping his sacred head allowed some of His hair to fall out of the garment to beautifully drape and shape His sacred face. He showed me both His hands. The beautiful hands gently held his draping royal blue silk garment from His face. So, it was intense beauty for I was viewing His face, His hair and both His hands. The rest of His body was completely covered in the deepest royal blue silk attire. Just too beautiful to accurately describe to you. The word beautiful does not justify what He truly looked like in this dream.

As I stood there looking at Him at a slight distance, I became immobile, unable to move at all. I was unable to move freely or turn my head even if I wanted to move, I did not have any ability to move.

Jesus standing in front of the church altar would not take His beautiful royal blue eyes off me. We just looked at each other and he never flinched His eyes for a moment. He had deep royal blue eyes that would instantly draw the soul to Him. Everything was so still. A perfect moment!

This is a moment of comfort. Jesus brings comfort. How may you ask? Here's is the how and I will explain it to you. Several months later or, to be precise, three months later, my first husband passed away on January 22, 1998. Shortly, after his death, as I went through his clothing, I recognized the white mid-sleeve shirt with the vertical blue stripes among his clothing. It was the same shirt I saw in the dream months prior to his death. So, the young man kneeling and praying intensely in the dream was my first husband! Jesus listening to the young man intense praying had his royal blue eyes on the upcoming young widow. His royal blue garments with His intense royal blue eyes gave the blessing of faith, hope and charity towards the widow. Jesus representing the church blesses the soul with the three theological virtues of the church: faith, hope and charity. For one must have faith in God, hope for the future and in charitable deeds that will radiate love, which will overcome adversity to continue the journey with the blessings of Our Royal King, Our Lord Jesus Christ who loves endlessly and full of mercy for all.

Dr. Ronda's Reflection:

Because we rarely see Jesus with our eyes, we can sometimes think He is not there when we pray. But He is!

It helps me to have a picture of Jesus on the wall in the room I pray in the most.

For You:

Try praying, at least once a day in front of a picture of Jesus on the wall or on a device.

Your thoughts or experiences:
Write them here:

Chapter Two

DREAM OF OUR LORD JESUS CHRIST

July 17, 2008

Seeing myself holding open a large gate, and across the way, directly opposite from me I see another person holding open another large gate: People are strolling slowly and calmly out of the double door chain link gate. The people are strolling out gradually through these large double chain link gates without any hesitation or rush.

Among these people are two priests walking side by side out of the gate. They look joyful and peaceful as they communicate among themselves. The people walking out of this gate I did not recognize but seem very calm. I saw myself holding onto one side of the gate wide open as I am dressed in a long white gown. As I mentioned earlier, the other side of the gate was being held open by another person. So, the person and I held the double door gates open for all these people to pass through.

Suddenly, as I have my hands directly on the gate, my hands drop abruptly from the gate.

I went into total shock because of what I was seeing in front of me.

What was I viewing that made me drop my hands abruptly from the gate? As I stood at the gate, I saw Our Lord Jesus Christ being held tightly at the arms by two people. There was one person on each side of Him grasping Him tightly as His hands were tied to his back. He was guided by these two people, as they walked with him squeezing tightly the arms of Our Lord, Jesus Christ.

Our Lord Jesus Christ had both His hands bonded or tied together tightly behind his back, as he had two people dressed in black walking, one on each side of him out of this gate.

Jesus has no garments only shredded coverage to lower extremities and took the resemblance of what He looks like on the cross.

Jesus was soiled and bloody. I could clearly see blood on His' Sacred Shoulders' and drops of blood on His forehead. He had a crown of very sharp thorns on His' Sacred Head.' Then something happens…

Jesus stopped walking and did not turn his body, as two people held onto him, but He turned his 'Sacred Head' to give me the deepest look as He was being taken out the gate by these two people. Jesus allowed his upcoming suffering, as he walked with these two people out the gate for even during suffering, he looks at everything through the eyes of love.

It was a shocking moment. For I was standing at a short distance viewing what these two people are doing to Him and at the same time looking straight at HIM. Jesus stood barefooted with two men holding on to Him.

Jesus and I just looked at each other with deep locking views. I did not have the ability to move or speak but to only to stand still to directly view Him.

The look He radiated was of no emotions of anger or sadness upon looking at me. "Why worry?" seemed to be the meaning of the look. I really cannot describe the look in words. The closest is He was trying to communicate with His eyes, "Why do you worry about Me? No need to worry, for I give you everything to continue and you still worry!"

I woke up and proceeded with my daily routine. A couple of days later, July 20, 2008, our family went to Sunday Mass. We received sad news about the Eucharist stolen from a local Perpetual Adoration Chapel during the week.

It took a while like several months for me to mention my dream in confession. I finally told a priest of the dream, He suggested spiritual guidance and said, "Today is the Exaltation of the Cross." I did not know; it was the Feast of the Exaltation of the Holy Cross.

In summarizing the dream, I learned the reason for the stealing of the sacred host. During Perpetual Adoration, some people stole the sacred host, and it was thought the motive was desecration. I believe the dream to be a precursor or foreshadowing with Jesus relaying the message not to worry about Him but to pray for the dark soul people who took him out of the perpetual adoration chapel. This desecration was like his suffering during the passion as he willingly gave his life to the perpetrators to save all of humanity from the sins of the world.

This is what I dreamed one night! The Savior of All!

Dr. Ronda Reflection:

Jesus has conveyed to many believers that He longs to save everyone, even those who follow the devil. Alicia's dream gave me the desire to pray more for such deluded persons.

For you:

If you have a prayer list, written, or only in your mind, add the word "Satanist," and pray for them and a change in hearten hearts.

Your thoughts or experiences:

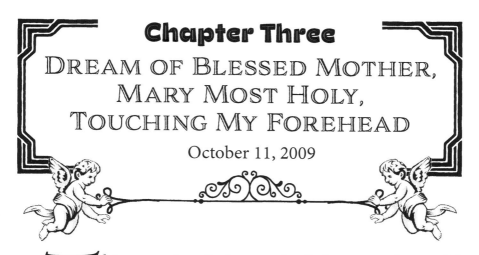

Chapter Three

DREAM OF BLESSED MOTHER, MARY MOST HOLY, TOUCHING MY FOREHEAD

October 11, 2009

This morning I dreamed of the most beautiful holy woman. It is none other than the Blessed Mother Mary for I dreamed her exactly as represented in the churches except with more brilliance and with flowing divine clear tears.

She came to me in a dream (interior vision) dressed in fine beautiful white lace that draped from her head to her feet with Mary's hands covered in her mantle. However, even with all the lace surrounding her I was able to view her entire face. Beautiful and graceful, as she takes her time to walk towards me in her long white lace attire with a huge colorful jeweled crown on her head.

What caught my attention immediately was the crown on her head. She had a huge, tall golden crown with the brilliant stones on top of her head. I took notice of the large crown because it was an exceptionally large gold colorful crown.

Gracefully and slowly, she walks towards me and stops in front of me. As I stood there before her, I noticed her height for she was taller than me. She looked brilliant.

Then she slightly leaned over me to touch my forehead.

In my dream, the entire time before she walked over, I

noticed she was crying from the beginning to the end of my dream. The tears got my attention because they did not look like regular tears for, they are divine. The tears were so clear that you could see right through the tears. They look like crystals falling from her eyes. She cried non-stop in front of me from the very beginning of my dream to the end of my dream.

As I watched her cry uncontrollably, I spoke to her, "Don't cry anymore! Just pray for all of us." The blessed mother nodded her head 'Yes.' I woke up.

Many years later, I discovered by accident while visiting a bookstore, *The Mystical City of God* by Venerable Mary of Agreda.

In summary, I would like to mention what I read regarding the jewels in heaven which can be found in Revelations 19-21. Even though this account is lengthy, I think you will enjoy Mary Agreda's vision. The brilliant stones are referred by Venerable Mary of Agreda's book, *The Mystical City of God* as she describes the jewels in detail by writing the following...

There are many precious stones such as Jasper, Sapphire, Chalcedony, Emerald, Sardonyx, Sardis, Chrysolite, Beryl, Topaz, Chrysoprase, Hyacinth and Amethyst. Heaven is made of these twelve precious stones and the twelve gates of heaven are actually twelve pearls. The streets are pure translucent gold and there is no temple" (Agreda 232).

Now, if you read this you probably think wow there is no temple, there is gold and precious stones, which is amazing. What is more amazing about this imagery of heaven is that it all relates to the one that said, "Yes" to God. It is Our Blessed Mother, Mary Most Holy.

How? Our Blessed Mother Mary is the tabernacle that housed the salvation of the world, Jesus Christ. Before I get to far into this of why is there no mention about a temple in heaven?

You may ask, "Why?" That is because 'there is no need for a temple, since God Almighty is the temple thereof, and the Lamb. So, again God is the temple, as Venerable Mary of Agreda states the following…

Now, God created all this and chose the holy city used to describe Mary, for God would adorn the foundations of the city's wall with all manner of precious stone, all these stones of virtues that none more rich or precious could ever be found. She represented the walls of the city, a dwelling place. The walls were strong and adorned with precious stones (Agreda 233).

Venerable Mary of Agreda's book, *The Mystical City of God* explains the meaning of the stones and I believe they coincide with Blessed Mother's golden crown filled with jewels in my dream, as the following…

"The first stone is the first foundation, and the jewel is Jasper. It's a representation of virtues and habits conceded and infused into Mary at her Conception and also given special privileges such as God endowing her sovereign power over the devil and evil. She was invested with actual authority from God to subdue the demons and send them to the hell.

Now, the second stone, my favorite, is the Sapphire, the color of the sky. This represents the serenity and tranquility of the gifts and graces of the most holy Mary.

The third stone is Chalcedony. This stone got its name from the country where it is found, and it is the color of the ruby. The hidden signification of this stone points to the holiness and power of the name of Mary. For she took her name from that part of the world, where she first came into being, calling herself a daughter of Adam, and her name, by the mere change of the accent signifies in Latin the collective oceans, for she was the ocean of the graces and gifts of the Divinity. God conceded to her most holy name the power to disperse the clouds of infidelity spread over earth, and destroy the errors of heresy, paganism, idolatry, and all uncertainty in matters of the Catholic faith. Invoking Mary's name brings light into everything.

Also, the city was of pure gold. It represents the interior of the soul of Mary, transparent like glass and pure gold. The city has no defects and the words given at the beginning to the most exalted work that God ever accomplished or will ever accomplish are in Latin "*Fiat mihi Secundum verbum tuum.*" In English, it simply is echoed throughout heaven and earth as Mary says, "Let it be done to me according to Thy word.

The fourth stone, an emerald, is a pleasant green. It represents Mary being most amiable and gracious in the eyes of God and his creatures.

The fifth stone, Sardonyx, is transparent, almost flesh-color with three different tints: dark below, whitish in the center, and like mother-of pearl. The mysterious significance is the stone's dark color points to the inferior and terrestrial portion, the white means purity of the soul of Mary.

The sixth stone is Sardis, is a transparent stone and it flashes like the clear flame of a fire. It is a symbol of the flame of divine love.

The seventh, Chrysolite, a stone with its color gold and it shows better by night than by day. It symbolizes the ardent love which Mary entertains for the Church militant, its ministers, and the law of grace in particular. She cooperated by her most burning love toward the salvation of the whole human race.

The eighth stone is Beryl. It is green and yellow color. It represents the singular faith and hope given to Mary in her conception and the power to endow her servants with fortitude and patience in the tribulations and difficulties of their undertakings.

The nineth stone is Topaz. It is transparent and of mulberry color. It represents the most honorable virginity of Mary, her mothership in regard to the Incarnate Word. She could obtain virtues and perseverance for all her devotees.

The tenth Stone, Chrysoprase, is the color of green with touches of gold. It signifies firm hope planted in the heart of Mary at her conception and that she might obtain the same firmness of hope for all her clients.

The eleventh stone, Hyacinth and is violet in color. It signifies the love of Mary for the Redemption of the human race.

The twelfth stone, amethyst's color is violet. This was given to her by God as a reward of her zeal in exalting and defending the glory and honor of God. She had an inherent power from the moment of her conception against all the devilish host, so that demons flee as the mere presence of Mary." (Agreda 232-240)

All these jewels are in the bible in Revelations 19-21 and Venerable Mary of Agreda defines the symbolism of the jewels in regarding Our Blessed Mary Most Holy, as the Tabernacle of God and the custodian of the crown of jewels represented on her holy mystical body. The mysteries of God are beautiful so enjoy them!

Dr. Ronda's Reflection:

Precious metals like gold and silver and precious stones have been used to adorn mankind's worship of God. Giving of our best to God is better than vanity and show.

For you:

What do jewels mean to you personally or in Church?

Your thoughts or experiences:

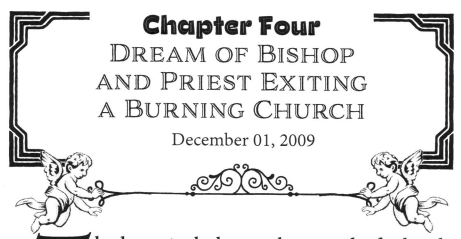

Chapter Four
DREAM OF BISHOP AND PRIEST EXITING A BURNING CHURCH
December 01, 2009

The dream took place on the grounds of a church. **I did not know the location of the church.** I was dressed in all white and standing in the middle of the street in front of this church. Simultaneously, I could see the inside of a church while I could also view the outside of this church at the same time. The church divided as such: all angles of the church inside and outside including the basement of the church are all viewable at the same time in my dream. So, as I stood in the middle of the street dressed in white, I could view the left side of the street and had the capacity to view the outside of the church. Now, on the right side of the street, I was able to view the inside of the church including the basement of the church. I could view of the church building inside and outside all at the same time. I have never been to or seen this church other than my dream. It soon became an unusual scary dream of a church burning.

First, I was in the basement of an exceptionally large church. There happened to be a marble altar in the center and to the left side a short distance from the altar, a group of priests gathered as they were talking to one another. Again, dressed in white, I was on the far right and away from everyone just overlooking all the action occurring in the church. Like overlooking everything and being present without anyone viewing me.

Suddenly, I see a fire starting at the altar and I start yelling in fright to all the priests gathering in the area, "Run! Hurry up! Run! Run!"

All the sudden, everything changed, I was now on the outside of the church in the middle of the street once again. I now see lots of people chatting with each other including sailors. It looked as if people were gathering outside for some kind of celebration. Now being outside, I was looking at the front of the church with lots of stairs at its entrance. It also has a huge fence around the area.

This is what I saw next: I saw its altar on fire with people at the altar catching on fire. I saw priests coming out and exiting the church. The first one to exit the church was a Bishop. The bishop exited the church carrying his staff, the crozier and in church attire with a large cross on his neck.

A line of priests was following neatly behind him and exiting the church in an organized manner. They are all going down the stairs and following one another to exit the church briskly due to the fire consuming the altar.

I woke up scared and started to pray about the dream.

A couple of weeks later while viewing the news on the internet, I learned of St. Mel's Cathedral in Longford, Ireland burning at 5:00 A.M., it was a couple of hours after Christmas Midnight Mass in 2009.

In summary, this may have been a precursor dream of the church burning. It could have been a spiritual calling to pray for all our brothers and sisters across the globe for safety. Prayers can help lessen the severity of tragedy by procuring the safety of its inhabitants such as during the fire within the church. We are grateful and thank God no one was hurt!

Dr. Ronda's Reflection:

Certainly, in the Old and New Testaments prophets had visions of future events. If most of us don't have prophetic or precursor dreams such as Alicia's, wouldn't it be good if whenever we read news of tragic happenings, we prayed for all involved instead of just feeling bad or indifferent?

Your thoughts or experiences:

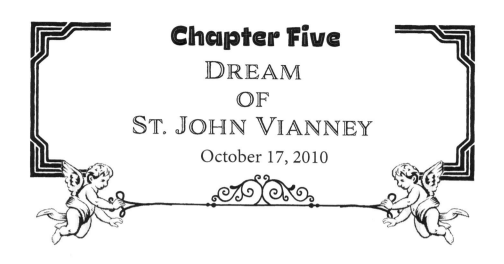

Chapter Five
DREAM
OF
ST. JOHN VIANNEY
October 17, 2010

It is beyond the imagination to dream of someone who lived from 1786 to 1859. Honestly, I did not know who St. Vianney was at the time of my dream. So, you can imagine my surprise waking up dreaming of a person that lived about one hundred sixty-one years ago. Even though I was a church goer, I never knew who he was and had never paid any attention of the famous St. John Vianney. The only reason I knew he was a saint in the dream is because his named spelled out clearly for me in my dream. St. Vianney's name was on the box placed up in the front of the church altar. I saw his name clearly in bold letters and in the same letter size written clearly as, 'ST. VIANNEY.' As a result of the dream, I learned who and what St. Vianney is for the Catholic faith.

I woke up wondering what in the world did I just dream and asked people who was St. Vianney? When I discovered St. Vianney's contribution to the Catholic church, as the patron saint of priests that just did it! I went into shock and could hardly believe it. I have never forgot any part of the dream since 2010.

More about the dream. In it, I entered a Catholic church with the location or the church being unfamiliar to me. There was no one in the church as I entered through the front doors, but I saw a box up in the front of the church.

Cautiously, while inside the church I looked around to see if there was anyone within the vicinity. I did not want to get into trouble for taking the curious initiative of walking up to the front of the altar for the sole purpose of opening the box in solitude in front of the altar. So, I made the decision to walk up to the front of the church, where the box laid before the altar. I looked once again to see if anyone was within the church before proceeding to open the lid on the box. There was no one else within the church except me and the box before me. I was now in front of the box that is in front of the altar. It clearly had a written label in bold letters on the box, ST. VIANNEY. All the letters of the name were of the same size and clearly identified the name of the saint.

I placed both my hands on the box lid. Cautiously opened the lid on the box labeled St. Vianney. This is what I saw when I opened the box.

It was unrecognizable human flesh, and it was neatly intact, as it lays within the red silk within the box. I picked up the organ laying within the red silk material with my bare right hand. I carefully carried the organ in my right hand and contemplated it for a while in my right hand. In other words, I just stared at it while it lay in my hands. I held the relic close to my face, so I could stare at St. Vianney. The relic fit perfectly in my hand. I looked around and hoping no one would see me holding St. Vianney in my hand.

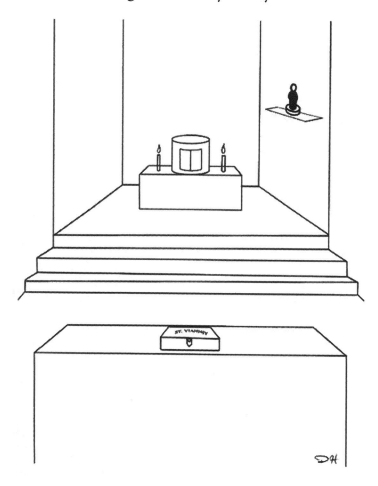

Then I took noticed a small brown empty shelf hanging on the wall to the side of the altar. What did I do next? I slowly and cautiously walked took St. Vianney in my hand with me up the steps of the altar. I placed the relic on the shelf nice and neatly, where it stayed perfectly intact without moving or falling from the shelf by the side of the altar. He stood perfectly intact on this shelf.

I woke up puzzled and wondering who is St. Vianney? Why was I dreaming about someone whose name was St. Vianney? As stated earlier, the only reason I clearly knew I was holding St. Vianney in my hand because I took him out of the box, which he was in, and his name was on the box in bold letters.

So, I will never forget the dream of St. Vianney and I hope you will learn more about him. Saints are actual people, flesh, and bones with all kinds of emotions, but they had a special grace from God to bring good news and hope to all people about the Kingdom of God. Naturally, I began to look up St. Vianney and found that his relics are in the town of Ars where he ministered to the people. My mind went into shock once again!

An interesting fact is that St. Vianney placed a statue of the blessed Virgin Mary in his church at Ars, France to consecrate his parishioners to the blessed mother. He specifically had all the names of his parishioners' names inscribe on a ribbon and placed within the inside of the heart of the statue in 1836.

The question now is why the spiritual dream came to me, Alicia Harley, in Corpus Christi, Texas, a great mystery. Maybe someday I will figure out what St. Vianney sought to communicate through this dream. It is a dream that I can never forget and have many questions about it. Some thoughts that have occurred to me are could St. Vianney want more intercession or prayers for religious vocations. What is St. Vianney really trying to tell me? What am I supposed to do with this kind of dream of a huge Saint in the Catholic church? Maybe it may be strictly just pray! Someday I will find out and if I pray to the saint, he will reveal his wishes in another dream. For now, we should all remain simple, humble, and pray as St. Vianney always did throughout his life.

Dr. Ronda's Reflection:

As a daily Mass Catholic surely, Alicia had heard of St. John Vianney on his annual feast days, but it had made no impression. I have written many books about the saints. Researching them in long biographies is so different than reading a paragraph in a Missal.

For you:

Why not try to find a lengthy description of each saint on the liturgical calendar on the web.

Your thoughts and experiences:

Chapter Six

DREAM
OF
ST. MARTIN OF TOURS

November 11, 2011

All there is to say about this morning is what a **revealing dream.** It was a dream of St. Martin of Tours. It was a spectacular dream!

The dream had no specific location because all I could see in the dream was a beautifully young holy child dressed in an ancient silk garment of gold standing right in front of me. It is way too beautiful to accurately describe the child wearing a long ancient silk garment in gold silk because he does not look like a modern-day child. I have never seen a child anywhere that looks this way. Never!

The child's hair had golden brown long locks of hair draping over his shoulder to the front of his body. The neatly fixed hair was pulled up perfectly while the other portion of the golden locks lay below the shoulders of the beautiful young child. The style of his hair may be slightly comparable to a gladiator's hairstyle, tight and smooth with the gathering it together, as it is pulled to the back of the head. The remaining portion of his hair, the long golden locks fell over to the front of his shoulders. The child's face was so perfect with the look of smoothest of skin with a neutral color, but not beige or totally white. It was naturally neutral in color. His face is incomparable to anything I ever seen on a fashion magazine or media. The shaping and lining of the lips were perfect. Again, the face and eyes of this child are shaped to perfection. The face looked angelic!

In the dream, the ancient child is looking straight at me as he stands, dressed in a long golden gown. What he did next was amazing!

The beautiful ancient child slowly raises in front of me both of his hands to eye level. He holds a large round white object with both his hands. I am assuming the large white object is the Eucharist.

Suddenly and neatly, he breaks the large white object, I

will call it 'The Eucharist' in front of me with no crumbs falling. There are no traces of any pieces falling! It is cut to perfection in a straight line with both his hands.

Next, he extends one of his arms straight out to offer me the other half of the large object (the Eucharist) he had cut in half. Again, I assume it is the Eucharist.

I quickly woke up!

I woke up wondering what did I just dream?

So, I revealed the dream to my husband, Doug Harley. He interpreted the dream to the best of his ability.

Doug told me, "Today is Friday, November 11 and it is Saint Martin of Tours Day." He continued saying, "Saint Martin of Tours gave up his garment when it was cold to a naked man needing clothing to keep him warm. St. Martin of Tours dreamed Jesus wearing the same half-cut cloak he had given away." Jesus told St. Martin, "Martin, who is still but a catechumen, clothed me with his robe. Truly I tell you, whatever you did for one of the least of these brothers and sister of mine, you did for me." So, my husband related my dream of Jesus breaking in half the Eucharist on the saint's celebrated day in the Church, as a revelation of St. Martin of Tours and Jesus within my dream. I made my husband cry when he finished figuring out the dream for me.

I never have prayed to Saint Martin of Tours. So, I wondered what does this has to do with me and why am I dreaming about a saint I know nothing about or ever heard of in my life.

So, I believe the ancient child I dreamed is the Child Jesus distributing himself by reenacting Martin of Tours actions before me to teach me the importance of giving through charity (love). Another thought maybe I did a good deed for

87

someone one day that Jesus in a dream reveals Himself to me. I do not know.

Amazingly, now forty-five years later, I looked upon my baptismal certificate and discovered that I was baptized at the Immaculate Conception Church in Rio Grande City, Texas on November 13, 1966. My baptism is close to Saint Martin of Tours 'day of November 11th.

Here are some things to know about Saint Martin of Tours. He was born in 316 or 336 AD in Savaria, now an area known as Hungary. He lived in France and became a soldier, monk, an exorcist and became Bishop of Tours.

Dr. Ronda's reflection:

I was not sure if the child was supposed to be St. Martin as a youngster, so I will comment instead on the famous St. Martin de Tours incident of giving his cloak to the poor man. I believe every time one gives money or possession to someone in need we will be blessed in heaven.

For you:

Who do you give to? When have you been the poor person?

Your thoughts and experiences:

Chapter Seven

DREAM OF A DEMONIC CHILD

November 12, 2011

A demonic child taunted me in my dream. I am walking in white in my dream. He was walking right next to me side by side, but I never stopped to talk to him throughout my dream. I was too busy walking and praying.

The demonic child waking next to me looks at me and says to me, "Stop it! Quit praying! You need to stop praying!"

I was in a hurry and replied to the demonic child, "Go away! I have no time to listen to you and I'm in a hurry."

Then loudly, while I was walking, I started to sing to God.

He quit taunting me when I sang a beautiful hymn to God.

So, in my dream I learned that all religious hymns sung by a person, whether at work or in worshiping, it does the following: In the presence of beautiful praises, singing beautiful hymns or chants, evil is silent and numb. This is what I learned from the dream. Again, evil is silent and numb when singing beautiful hymns or chants to God.

So, my advice to you is sing loudly to God.

Dr. Ronda's reflection:

I loved the message of this dream. I am going to start singing aloud or in my heart whenever negative thoughts that could be from evil spirits are clouding my mind.

For you:
Try the same as I will do.

Your thoughts and reflections:

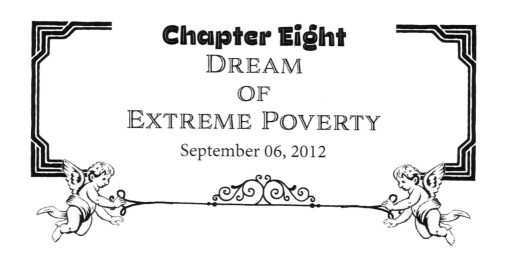

Chapter Eight
DREAM
OF
EXTREME POVERTY
September 06, 2012

It was an unusually large place where nuns were staying with children. A nun told me, "I am Sister Teresa."

She added, "I am going to leave to attend to the poorest of the poorest. Take me there!" I told her, "Yes" and together we walked out of the large building.

However, I told her to wait up for me because she had left all her important items behind, so I went back inside the building. Now, the building took a change, it was quite different and not at all a normal room. It was very elegant. I saw beautiful furniture, cushions, carpet from one area to the next area. So, I looked around and started walking back outside of the room.

As I stepped outside the door of the building, I saw passengers on a train, and it was children without their parents sitting in a cargo of a train looking out the window. The young children were about seven to eleven years of age. The children had dirty hair and clothing that was torn up.

A fire engine followed the train, which I thought was an unusual thing to see in my dream. So, I started to walk and

saw a pile of ashes. The ashes are high and smoldering, just like a fireplace. I got close to the ashes to see what was on top of the ashes. It was a cross.

I saw a large wooden cross with the Infant Jesus laying on top of the cross. The cross HE was on laid on top of the ashes. I stood there looking at him because he started to move slightly, as if HE is in pain. The Infant Jesus in agony is moving on the wooden cross looks at me and speaks in a command as he says, "Go and find someone to come and help, and be with me!"

I turned around to look for someone and could not find anyone in the area. There was a fence encircling the area. So, I ended up yelling for someone to help but there was no one to help the Infant Jesus asking for help on the cross in pain.

An update or personal thought on the dream for I learned a shocking truth around April 2022, while at a Legion of Mary's local group at a church.

Sister Teresa of Calcutta became a discussion at the group

meeting. I went into shock when it was mentioned Sister Teresa taught wealthy girls in a beautiful building. In remembering my dream of the beautiful building and the nun, Sister Teresa I went into shock while sitting in this room for I
did not know this about her at all. So, is this considered a
precursor dream for I dreamt the train, a wealthy building,
Sister Teresa and poor children? I do not know. I also did
not know much about Sister Teresa or Mother Teresa of Calcutta until now. In summarizing, D. Jeanene Watson's short
book, *Teresa of Calcutta Serving the Poorest of the Poor*, I was
shocked to find out that her real name was Agnes. Agnes became a nun, who would later change her name to Sister Teresa. She became a teacher to top elite government officials'
children of Bengal and of the British. The private school was
on top of a mountain away from poverty in the lower area
of Bengal and Calcutta. Sister Teresa would travel by train
and much later traveled through all the slum areas of Calcutta. It was horrifying as she saw children in poverty and
starving, even an old man who claimed to have never slept
on a mattress became happy to know that he would now be
able to die in one, as per Watson. Sister Teresa saw one child
who could no longer cry from hunger, so the small child laid
helpless in an infested area of rodents in silence. No matter
what situation, children are innocent and require the help of
adults to survive in the world.

The poverty is extreme in many countries and it may also
be felt in a soul when it lacks moral and authentic compassion of those suffering all kinds of poverty. We can assist
all of our brothers and sisters to fight all types of poverty
through compassion, prayer and charitable works.

Let us give now Saint Teresa of Calcutta the last words in
this chapter in regards to poverty among all mankind, as she
stated the following, "They starve in silence. If they die it is

not because God doesn't care for them, but because you and I don't give. We are the tools of love in the hands of God. Give them bread, give them clothing, help heal them and teach them. You'll be helping Christ."

Dr. Ronda's reflection:

This interior vision (dream) will be used as a sample at the beginning of the book of Alicia's dreams so you can get a sense of what they are like. What are your thoughts?

Your thoughts and reflection:

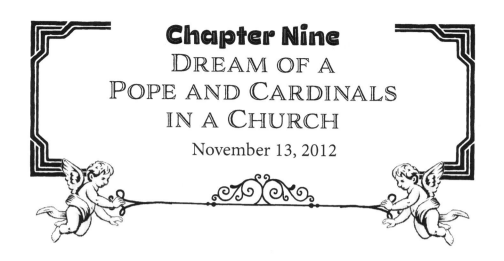

Chapter Nine
DREAM OF A POPE AND CARDINALS IN A CHURCH
November 13, 2012

On this day, a total solar eclipse took place since it crossed international waters. It is now 5:40 A.M. on Tuesday, November 13, 2012, and before introducing my dream to you, I will say that I think it may have been a precursor dream.

In my dream, there was a church with a dome shaped room. It was fully elaborate inside with lots of heavy waxed lit up candles. It looked like a private chapel. On the altar, there were two lit up candles. In this room, which I call a private beautiful chapel, I saw a kneeling Pope before the tabernacle praying with all his heart.

The Pope dressed in all white and was the only person in the room praying before the tabernacle. However, in my dream I was in the same room dressed in white, at a distance, just watching him pray. Simultaneously, I can view the private chapel where a Pope was praying and, also, the other adjacent room of Cardinals gathering to pray with one another. In the adjacent room there are men in red caps on their heads gathering to pray, I will assume they were Cardinals. They all gathered to pray, before meeting with one another in the adjacent room. So, as the men in the red caps situated themselves by kneeling, one of the men in a red cap said to the rest of them, "Let's all pray to be free us from any distractions." The Pope was in the opposite room praying in front of the tabernacle, ALONE.

Suddenly, the deepest evil voice coming from the adjacent room where all the men in the red caps were together resonates as it announces, "I AM NOW TAKING OVER!"

The Pope heard the evil voice. It resonated into his private chapel. Upon hearing this, the Pope quickly got up from the kneeler in fright to see what was going on around him. He was extremely scared of this resonating evil voice. He removed himself from the kneeler and turned around to walk briskly and quickly from the private chapel. He started to walk briskly in this long exit from his private chapel, on an illuminated path or hallway. The long-illuminated path had lite up sconces down the wall of the long hallway.

In my dream I followed him with a short distance between both of us, as we quickly exited out through the hallway and briskly towards the exit from the chapel. The only illumination was the light from the sconces on the wall. However, as we passed the first lit up sconce on both sides of the wall, each one instantly diminished itself as we passed. As, the Pope passes the second sconces, they diminished as well, while we briskly walked past the sconces. The Pope made a quick turn to look back and so did I only to see total darkness left behind us. There is no light behind us except

a little from the candles on the altar. The men in the red caps were left in a totally dark room.

So, is it possible I dreamed of the Pope exiting the church in a dream three months before the official announcement to the world of his retirement? Is this what is called a precursor dream?

Concerning the dream, I would like to ask the reader to pray for all priests, for our Pope and for the Church. It is our hope to have more, more and more good and holy priests; so therefore, we shall continue to pray with strong faith for religious vocations.

Dr. Ronda's reflection:

There were many reactions to events in the Vatican after the retirement of Pope Benedict. See my book "The Crisis in the Church" for my thoughts. Certainly, praying for all concerned is good. Unless you are a canon lawyer or a theologian reading websites about the crisis can lead to anxiety and even despair. It is better mostly to pray.

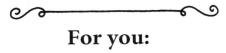

For you:

Cling to those priests you trust most and follow their advice when in doubt.

Your thoughts and experiences:

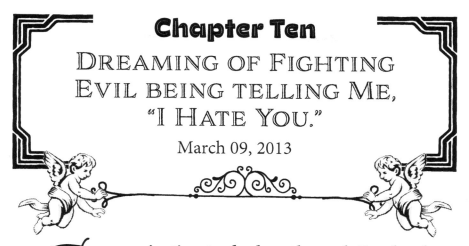

Chapter Ten

DREAMING OF FIGHTING EVIL BEING TELLING ME, "I HATE YOU."

March 09, 2013

Communication took place through Facebook, as I asked a few people on my page, "Do you ever have weird dreams like this weird one? Just Feel Like Sharing." I did get two responses from two different people, "Wow!" and "I believe you have a gift!" but I NEVER got the response I wanted to hear, "Yes, we do dream this way."

It had just been a couple of months since we had moved into our new home. My daughter in her upstairs bedroom had a nightmare and ran downstairs into my room frightened. She fell asleep for a couple of hours before getting over the nightmare and returning to her room.

I fell back to sleep after my daughter went back to her room. Believe it or not? I continued her dream from where my daughter ended her nightmare. How I continued the dream I do not know, but all I can say that I picked up my daughter's dream where she ended her nightmare. It was darn scary. We discussed it the following morning. However, as I am writing this today, I think she will not remember the dream. I am glad if she does not, but I do remember the dream very well.

The dream started with my daughter dreaming of someone knocking on our front door. It was an unpleasant dark figure. She never opened the door and that ended her dream. It was enough to frighten her. She woke up and ran downstairs to my room. I told her not to be scared for it was only a dream.

I fell back to sleep after she returned to her room to fall back asleep.

Now, this is my dream… Someone, an unpleasant dark figure was knocking on our front door, I continued to open the front door. It was an unpleasant and horrifying dark figure.

The person at the door, a dark figure completely dressed in black was a horrifying site. As I opened the door, it stepped into the house. A fight broke! The black figure and I started to fight and ended up on the floor rolling around in a huge fight. We were fighting and rolling all over the floor inside my house.

As the black figure and I were fighting, I managed to stop rolling around with it and pinned its arms down. I held both arms down while it laid flat on the floor in a helpless motion but not willing to look at me. Its head was looking the other way as I sat on top of its body as I pinned down the figure on my floor.

It did not look at me, but I was on top of the figure pinning the figure down. The figures arms stretched out onto the floor. I was holding on to the arms while I straddled myself over the figure.

Suddenly, the black figure turned around to show me its face. I went into shock! It was horrifying and evil. A demonic face!

Then the face for a second modified itself into someone

I knew very well, and the name will remain nameless in respect for her privacy before changing back to the evil demonic face.

I pinned it down with my weight, I asked the evil dark figure, "Why are you bothering me?" It responded, "I never liked you! I HATE YOU!" I quickly woke up!

When I woke up the next day I went about my business. I was washing dishes downstairs when my daughter ran downstairs to make an announcement "Mom, (nameless person) just died a couple of minutes ago at the hospital and it is on Facebook. She has been sick and in the hospital for a couple of days."

It was a shocking moment because this is the same person whose face was revealed to me on the face of the evil dark figure, as I got a glimpse of in the horrifying dream. I knew the person! I did not attend her funeral.

In summary, it does not mean this nameless person is evil since this is a dream. I did pray for the person. So, it is important to pray for all souls because we do not know another person's sin; therefore, it is wise to say prayers for souls in purgatory at all Masses and rosaries. Maybe God grants people the grace to reach out during the last agonizing hours in life for strong prayers. Honestly, I do not know.

Dr. Ronda's reflection:

"Love your enemies." "Pray for those who trespass against you." Since our own forgiveness and salvation depends on forgiveness, we must pray for anyone we think hates us personally or as part of a group, such as in political enmity.

For you:

Have you ever known that anyone hated you? If so, pray for that one and any others you think of.

Your thoughts and experiences:

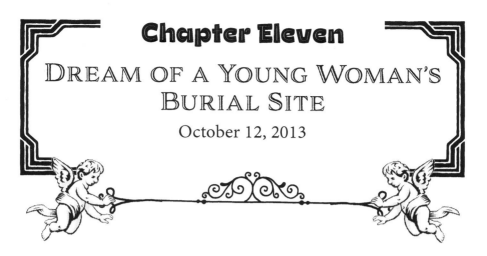

Chapter Eleven

DREAM OF A YOUNG WOMAN'S BURIAL SITE

October 12, 2013

The dream takes place out on a highway with some construction happening on the road. Driving in car on this long busy interstate, the road got rerouted due to the construction. The other road was for cars to move onto and drive on it. Now, to the side of this road, a bumpy white gravel road a short cut and a deterrent from the busy construction of the highway, I saw two cars driving out of a gate down the road, as it was left wide open.

The white gravel rocks on the road made an interesting drive. It was a bumpy road and along the driving path it had a barbed wire fence, held up with old wood posts.

Suddenly, a young woman appeared within a short distance standing in the middle of the graveled road.

The young girl wore dark jeans, dark flat shoes, a long sleeve shirt. The top portion of her long hair was pulled back. It hung down to her waist. She could not have been more than twenty-five years old. She had a natural looking face without cosmetics to hide her natural looks as a young adult.

I stopped the car. The young girl was standing in front of

my car. The girl turned around to start walking in front of my car, to guide me to a location. She wanted me to follow her, and I proceeded to follow the young girl.

I began to follow the girl who was walking about two to three feet in front of my car. Finally, she made an abrupt stop in front of a barbed wire fence post. Strangely, she sat down on the white gravel rock, right in front of the fence post.

She sat upright in front of the fence post with both her legs stretched out about a half a foot away from the post.

Then I see the following: The young girl quickly started to cover her lower torso with the gravel rocks. She covered both her feet, ankles, lower legs, knees, upper legs completely with the white gravel and then slowly laid herself down. Then she started covering her hips and upper torso completely with the rocks.

I woke up! I told my husband about the girl, and he asked if she told me her name. I said, "No, but I think she was showing me where she was buried."

Many years later, I had a similar dream of such a young woman and her burial but this time she told me her name. She softly told me her name, but I told my husband, "It sounded like Justin. I do not know. All I know it starts with a J." He told me was it "Julie." I said, "Yes. That is, it! Her name is Julie."

My husband told me, "A friend of my siblings was named Julie. She passed away when we were young kids." He told me he did not know much about her since he was not close to her like his siblings, and they were all very young. Julie died tragically in a vehicle.

Trying to interpret the dream, I would say that the young woman had a grace that may have allowed her to reach out to people to pray for her. Is she in purgatory? I do not have the answer but dreaming of a dead person twice and learning of a name could signify a suffering soul who is requesting a Mass or prayers.

My question is why me and not the family or families who may have known her? So, we did not hesitate to pray for her. My husband and I prayed for someone named Julie. May she rest in peace!

Dr. Ronda's reflections:

Years ago, I read about a mystic in Europe who was given a ministry of praying for souls in purgatory. People would visit her and talk about a person's life, and they would pray until the mystic was "told" from heaven that the person's soul had gone from purgatory to heaven.

For you:

Make a list of people who you know who have died and pray for their souls.

Your thoughts and experiences:

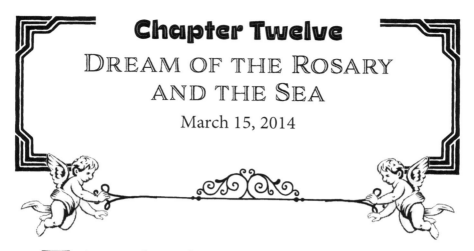

Chapter Twelve

DREAM OF THE ROSARY AND THE SEA

March 15, 2014

It is neat how the mind works during a dream. It was a beautiful day! I was in an area filled with families and children. Everyone was having a wonderful day with children running around enjoying their day.

Suddenly, my dream switched over to where I was now walking in the area with people praying the rosary for it was a large crowd of people. There was a man, not a child, who was walking beside me, He told me "You are praying too loud, and I need you to STOP praying!" Ignoring him, I continued praying the rosary with a loud voice.

The man in my dream got upset and so angry, as he said to me, "I told you to STOP praying! There is no need to pray loud. So, stop praying, NOW!"

Then I see the following: I see an area that was once surrounded with beautiful water take a change. Now the ocean along with boats in the water start to come onto the shore. Almost like all the water of the ocean was being emptied into the area or like a tsunami in the area where the families with their children were having a good day. In my dream, I yelled out to the people, "Get out and run, this is your chance!"

However, I continued to pray out loud. Frustrated, annoyed and angry at the man, I turned around to tell him, "Don't you know that this area has been claimed by the people for God."

The man ceased bothering me, He turned around to leave the area.

Then I saw everything go into a reverse motion or backwards into its normal beginning of the day. Everything went back into its place, including the water and the boats. The sea returned to normal, and it was once again a beautiful day.

In interpreting this dream, I thought that the sea symbolizes, "people, multitudes, nations and tongues." The boat represents the church. The bible verse found in Mark 4:1, "On another occasion he began to teach by the sea. A very large crowd gathered around him so that he got into a boat on the sea and sat down. And the whole crowd was beside the sea on land." The symbolism shows the church stepping into the boat, as all people await to hear His word. The secular world drawn by the power of prayer around the area, the Church, where Jesus sat and waits until ALL will enter the church.

It is impossible to resist Him even if living in a secular world because the rosary will pull people from the secular world. I believe it will be the rosary that will draw or pull souls into HIS church. We are all welcomed guest in HIS home, as his mother, Blessed Mother Mary gathers us in the prayers of the rosary to bring us to Jesus. 'To Jesus through Mary!'

Dr. Ronda's refection:

Many Catholic visionaries tell Catholics to pray for sinners, especially with the rosary. I have prayed it every day for some fifty years.

For you:

If you don't like praying the rosary or only pray it seldom, try looking up meditations on the rosary. There are many ways to pray it, some you might really enjoy.

Your thoughts and experiences:

Chapter Thirteen
DREAM OF THE SOULS PLEADING FOR HELP!
May 2014

My dreams are very intense at times such as this dream I am presenting to you now; it is about the suffering of families in hunger due to the extremes of poverty? Is it really about hunger? Could it be the souls in purgatory or the dead begging for help from the faithful? You decide.

Here is the dream…

The dream starts off with me strolling through the middle of this city street in a long plain white gown with long sleeves, it ties at the top of my chest area. There were no driven cars in the area, but I walked down the street slowly in disbelieve and amazement of what I was viewing on this street.

There was people to the left side and people on the right side of the street one after another in many rows down the street all in extreme poverty.

The right side of the street had people sitting on the floor waiting for food, it continued on and on with more people right behind one another waiting in this extreme poverty. Almost what you would see in a soup kitchen line but with an extreme amount of people waiting for what seemed to be unavailable food.

There was a whole family living in a car for there was no home for them to reside but only a car. I saw the father in grief with several sorrowful children in his car just looking out their window from their vehicle watching me. They are silent but their pain is upon their face for I am able to see their pain on their faces.

The left side of the street had people in cardboard boxes living in them. They had no cars but settle for whatever they could find to stay together with their loved ones, a cardboard box.

As I walked down the middle of the street in shock, I clearly viewed a mass of people by the hundreds: to the left side and on the right side of the public sidewalk of the street in this dire poverty. The souls were in poverty, as I slowly walking down the street was viewing endless amount of people in extreme poverty on both sides of this street.

Without ever being noticed in my dream, it felt as I could actually be viewing inside the private lives of these people, as they sat there both to the left and right of the street. They were showing me how much they are suffering from the evils presented to them in their current life or past life. Yes, it was a journey into the inside of people's life of all ages, genders, races for poverty in materialism or even in the inside of a soul will not deter itself, as it picks up and sweeps whom it wishes within its current path or past, if the souls do not fill up with the fruits offered by God. For even if the person is poor but has much fruit, it will have a radiating enlightenment within its growing soul.

I saw children and families dressed in pajamas crying longing for food and a home. I walked down the street and continued seeing people pleading and begging for help;

however, they never moved from the area on street (side-walk) or space they occupied on the sidewalk of the street. They pleaded from the space they occupied as I walked by them, crying and reaching out their hands but never allowed to leave the area where they sat or stood on the sidewalk. All they could do is beg and cry with sorrowful eyes, as I pass in astonishment by them down the street.

I just continued walking slowly by them watching all the agony coming from both sides of the city street.

I woke up my husband and cried about it. This is what I dreamt one night.

Dr. Ronda's reflection:

A wonderful dream. We know that extreme poverty exists in our world. It is much worse than when someone we know says they are poor but really means that they can't buy everything they might want! I like to try to live as simply as possible to have more to give to the poor. I like to give to the Missionaries of Charity founded by Mother Teresa, because then I know it gets to the poorest of the poor. However, others I know give lots of money to people they know who are poorer even if not destitute.

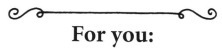

For you:

Consider with each thing you want to buy whether it is needed or simply something attractive that is not at all as needed as food for the poor to whom you could give that money. Consider given away lots of things you don't use so that the poor can find them cheap at second hand shops.

Your thoughts and experiences:

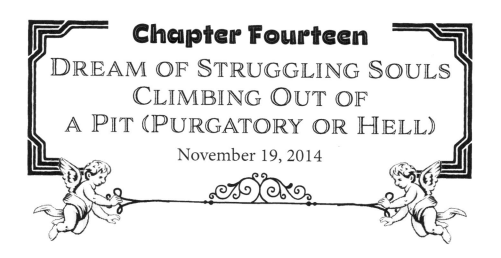

Chapter Fourteen
DREAM OF STRUGGLING SOULS CLIMBING OUT OF A PIT (PURGATORY OR HELL)

November 19, 2014

Another strange dream this day. I dreamt of seeing in the middle of a street, a large hole in the ground. It resembled a large crater in the ground left after an earthquake or mud slide. where there it is an endless opening section in the ground of the earth. The unusual thing within this dream is I am standing dressed in white overlooking this large crater in the ground. There is a

young man standing next to me dressed in white assisting me or showing me what is taking place within this large opening crater on the earth.

As I stood on the street or ground, I was looking down into this large and endless crater in the ground.

This handsome young man, who was all dressed in a long white gown standing to the side of me on the street looks to be a guide showing me all what is happening below us as we both look down into the crater. Noticing he was barefooted with watery eyes, he stood next to me without speaking to show me what was going on within this large hole in the ground.

As the young man and I stood next to each other at the edge of this large hole in the ground, I looked down into this large hole within the earth. This is what I saw within this large hole in the ground.

I saw people within this deep endless open dirty rocky wall within this pit. I was not able to see their faces for they consumed themselves with the endless struggle to get out of the pit, so they could not raise their heads to look up at us for they are trying to climb up a woven rope that has been thrown down this crater. These people were in this open pit dressed in torn up brown paper sack (paupers) clothing. I could see a man in the middle between two women desperately trying to climb out of the pit; however, there are more people in the pit under these three people. These three people were the ones higher up and closer to the edge of the hole but could never pull out of it no matter how hard they tried to get out of the hole. All the people in the crater never advanced on the rope placed down the crater to climb out of it. It was impossible!

These people were desperately trying as hard as they

could to climb out but never managed to climb out; even though, they were at the top, yet never reaching the top of the hole to get out of it. These three particular people were climbing at the same level yet above the others in the pit, but never reach the top of the pit, as they are trying to climb the side of the deep open pit of dirt. I saw other people below them struggling to climb out of this pit. It was an extremely difficult task. They never progressed climbing out of this open pit in the ground. I raised my head from looking down at the pit of struggling souls who desperately tried to climb out of the horrible pit.

I looked up from seeing the souls suffer in their struggle to get out of the pit and turned my head to look at the young man standing right next to me. He had short brown hair with fair complexion with clear brown eyes. He looked to be around his late twenties or early thirties. His eyes held a deep sadness in his eyes, and he looked at me with teary eyes from witnessing the struggling souls so desperately trying to climb out of the pit of dirt. We stood there without speaking looking at the struggling souls. He wanted me to see the immense and endless suffering going on in this horrible pit.

I woke up! What did I dream and such a strange dream? I posted this dream into Facebook.

A person posted a long comment that made an impress on me, "There is a neat video on YouTube called 'Seven Columbian Youth Vision of Hell' or something like it. I really was saddened by it, especially the part where there was a section of hell for people who know God's laws, but they did not follow them." This is what one person stated on my Facebook comment on this dream.

I have yet to look up the video mentioned in the comment but may sometime to see what it entitles and if it may

119

point to an explanation in the dream. I will tell you Dr. Ronda thinks these souls are not in Purgatory but in Hell for they never are able to get out of the pit.

So, was I being shown the struggling souls in Purgatory or in Hell?

I do not know the answer, but we must pray for the souls in purgatory for you cannot pray for the souls in Hell since it is too late for those souls. However, souls in purgatory can pray for us here on earth as we pray for them to relieve them of their suffering in purgatory. Souls tormented in these two places are vastly different for in one area such as purgatory, the souls await our prayers to exit out of this place into a more heavenly realm. In Hell, the souls cannot be prayed for because they have been condemned; therefore, no prayers will be received or needed for souls in Hell. These two places are both a place and a condition for the souls. Some souls suffering in purgatory are allowed to reach out to people on earth through apparitions or dreams in order pray for their release from purgatory if they are in purgatory.

Dr. Ronda's reflection:

I feel blessed that there is purgatory, for most of us are not saints to go right to heaven but not so evil as to belong in hell.

For you:

Let us always pray for the souls in purgatory.

Your thoughts or experiences:

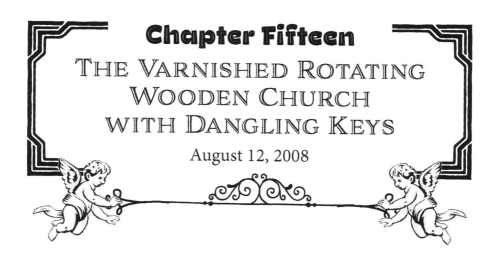

Chapter Fifteen

THE VARNISHED ROTATING WOODEN CHURCH WITH DANGLING KEYS

August 12, 2008

This dream will seem to be out of chronological order, but intentionally placed here for it will deal with a series of dreams of the saint Padre Pio following this one. Enjoy the saint Padre Pio dreams for they are remarkably interesting.

This dream starts as I am taking a drive going up a twisting road mountain. The road was very narrow with a twisting round street road. As I drove up this mountain, there were people passing me by in motorcycles and driving in cars. Driving on this road, which has a habitation of very green plants as I traveled up the mountain in this winding road.

Finally, upon reaching the top of the mountain, I walk into their gift shop. In the gift shop there was a particular item of interest to me. It was a very unusual jewelry box. It was a varnished hand carved wood, which rotated, and it is in the shape of a church. It had a lot of little dangling keys within the outside of its keyhole.

Opening the varnished box in the church, I found lots of pieces of brilliant colorful jewelry with a multitude of assorted colors within the box. I was able to turn or rotate the beautiful wood varnished box in shape of a church. Also, it had more places within the box for more jewelry. There seem to be a ticket with a price of thirty something dollars, but the lady in my dream said, "It is the only one left." I told the lady, "I will take the varnished box of the church."

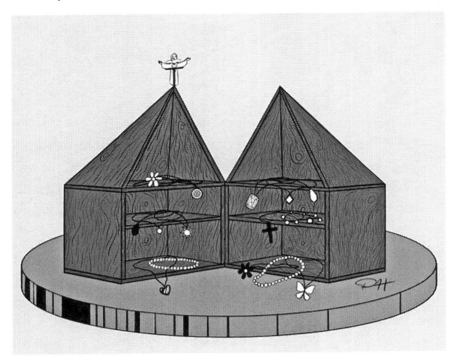

Further to the right, I saw a glass case display and looking into it, it was relics of no other than Padre Pio. I asked the lady within the gift shop, "Are these relics second or third-class relics?" She said, "I do not know." Each of the cards had a distinctive mark because it had a small fragment of a bone attached with a particular prayer on it. I took the initiative to open a small novena prayer card and it had prayers and intentions to Saint Padre Pio. In my dream, I overheard a conversation of the people saying, "Padre Pio knew he was going to die, but he would have loved to remain here to heal the people." I have never prayed to Padre Pio. I wondered why I would dream this saint. What was on the prayer card for I did not bother to read all of it in my dream? In my dream, instantly I got flashes of images of what he looked like after he died laying in his coffin. I woke up!

Dr. Ronda's reflection:

I love Padre Pio. What a life-story. So persecuted and so radiantly holy.

For you:

Read an account of Padre Pio's life or watch the movie on Padre Pio.

Your thoughts or experiences:

SERIES OF
SAINT PADRE PIO DREAMS

Several dreams of Padre Pio will follow one another, and these are dreams I will never forget about this saint. Since these dreams, I do pray to him on occasion, since I do believe he blessed me in a dream and performed a personal healing for an ICU patient. Now, I will write about the dreams to show how Padre Pio reaches out to people. He intercedes in people's lives without any barriers. This is proof of God reaching out to us through whatever means as he gifts the Capuchin Friar, Padre Pio, the power to intercede for his people with a great love. Padre Pio pray for us!

Here is a prayer for all of us:

"Stay with me, Lord, for it is necessary to have You present so that I do not forget You. You know how easily I abandon You.

Stay with me Lord, because I am weak, and I need Your strength, so that I may not fall so often.

Stay with me Lord, for You are my life, and without You, I am without fervor.

Stay with me Lord, for You are my light, and without you, I am in darkness.

Stay with me Lord, to show me Your will.

Stay with me Lord, so that I hear Your voice and follow You.

Stay with me Lord, for I desire to love you very much, and always be in Your Company.

Stay with me Lord, if You wish me to be faithful to You.

Stay with me Lord, for as poor as my soul is, I want it to be a place of consolation for You, a nest of Love.

Stay with me, Jesus, for it is getting late, and the day is coming to a close, and life passes, death, judgment, eternity approach. It is necessary to renew my strength, so that I will not stop along the way and for that, I need You. It is getting late and death approaches. I fear the darkness, the temptations, the dryness, the cross, the sorrows. O how I need You, my Jesus, in this night of exile.

Stay with me tonight, Jesus, in life with all its dangers, I need You.

Let me recognize You as Your disciples did at the breaking of bread, so that the Eucharistic Communion be the light which disperses the darkness, the force which sustains me, the unique joy of my heart.

Stay with me Lord, because at the hour of my death, I want to remain united to you, if not by Communion, at least by grace and love.

Stay with me Jesus, I do not ask for divine consolation because I do not merit it, but the gift of Your presence, oh yes, I ask this of You.

Stay with me Lord, for it is You alone I look for, Your Love, Your Grace, Your Will, Your Heart, Your Spirit, because I love You and ask no other reward but to love You more and more.

With a firm love, I will love You with all my heart while on earth and continue to love You perfectly during all eternity. Amen.

(A Prayer of Padre Pio After Holy Communion).

While on my way out of Mass this morning on December 30, 2013, I found a book on the floor, which no one bothered to pick up. So, I picked up the book and placed it on a table within the church, but a small piece of paper fell out, entitled 'A Prayer of Padre Pio After Holy Communion.' Finding this paper with the prayer written on it made me think Padre Pio must want me to really pray to him, since I have dreamed him several years prior to finding this prayer. Is this the revealing prayer? As far-fetched as it sounds could the prayer finally be revealed to me? Is it perhaps because God slowly reveals to us one thing at a time and not all at once? Is this the prayer from a dream that written in chapter sixteen encased with the relic that I could not read within the dream? Just a thought. It is a mystery to me.

Dr. Ronda's reflection:

What a beautiful prayer! All of us can pray it with profit.

For you:

Try saying this prayer after Holy Communion for a while.

Your thoughts and experiences:

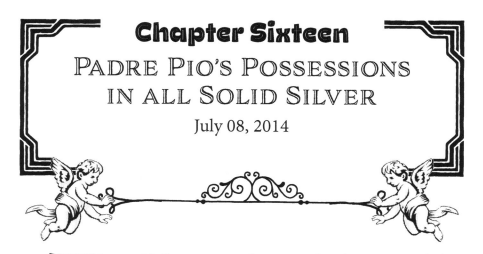

Chapter Sixteen
PADRE PIO'S POSSESSIONS IN ALL SOLID SILVER
July 08, 2014

Abeautiful, strange dream! The location of this dream took place in an unknown large library. It had tall shelves filled with books from its top to the very bottom of them. What caught my attention are several bounded deep brown leather books about waist high on the shelf within this reachable section of the bookshelf. These books are about five inches wide by seven inches in length.

I grabbed a leather book on this shelf. The book had a large cross emblem on its front of the deep brown leather. It was a thick book and comparable to a Psalm book. In opening the book up to my amazement within the pages laid a vacuumed clear tight plastic sealed up bag within the book.

The contents of the sealed vacuumed bag contained a prayer. I was so shocked in my dream that I did not bother to read the prayer.

What I noticed are the following three items within the inside of the sealed vacuum bag: a large silver cross, a silver medallion, and a silver rosary. The entire contents were of solid silver and within this airtight vacuumed bag.

The large clear sealed vacuum bag with its contents had a

label on it with the name Padre Pio written on it.

I thought "Why is this here?" and "Should it be displayed somewhere within this library." So, I looked around the library and noticed there is hardly anyone within the library. It was me and about three people, but the three were at tables reading books. It was extremely quiet.

In my dream, no one noticed me as I stood there in amazement with the contents of this open book in my hands.

So, I posted this dream to Facebook to talk about the dream of the saint. I asked how many times do you dream of saints from long ago? Let me know? I also wondered if Padre Pio was the saint of the day in the Catholic calendar and found that he was not the saint of this day. Here are well-known facts of Padre Pio:

- Born on May 25, 1887.
- Stigmata received on September 20, 1918.
- Died on September 23, 1968, at eighty-one years old.
- Beautified by Pope John Paul II on May 02, 1999.
- Canonized on June 16, 2002.

Dr. Ronda's reflection:

It is so much part of human life to possess precious things. I cherish such mementos of beloved dead family members such as my husband's favorite shirt or a daughter's handmade rosary.

For you:

What do you cherish of this sort?

Your thoughts and reflections:

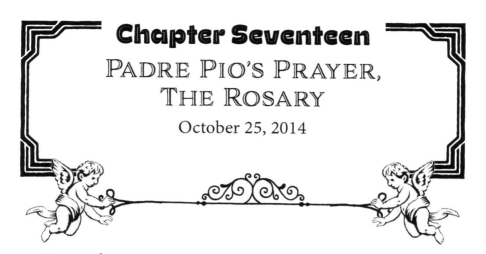

Chapter Seventeen

PADRE PIO'S PRAYER, THE ROSARY

October 25, 2014

This dream has a lot of nature surrounding it. The dream centers on a beautiful morning. There is a field with tall grass out in the middle of nowhere but within a short distance of what looks like a forest of tall trees surround this grassy field.

An open field with tall grass is where I found myself standing dressed in white looking around asking myself, "Where am I?" "What is this?" "What am I doing here standing in the middle of this field with lots of tall grass?"

In this open field, I saw the large green trees at a distance. Further down the open field, I observed a bunch of people gathering to pray with Bibles and rosaries. Startled by the people in the field, I quickly became curious and wanted to know what they are doing praying in the middle of an empty field. So as I am approaching the people by walking over to them, I was then distracted by someone I have seen before in a previous dream.

The person I saw was a priest dressed in white with a brown rope belt around his waist. It was no other than the famous Padre Pio with a rosary in his hand.

He was ready to say a Mass, but before the Mass he was

walking quickly towards me.

In his hand, he had a brown rosary and handed it over to me. I took the rosary from him his hand and turned around to walk away from the area. When I looked back once again to see the people, I found out that they were all gone. It is now a vacant field.

So, I started walking with the rosary he gave me. There now appeared two young girls in front of me as they lead the way and guide me from the field.

I woke up wondering what this dream meant, and why dream of the famous saint Padre Pio, again. What was he trying to tell me? What is the urgency of him coming to me in dreams? Maybe it would be revealed who knows but I will pray.

Prayer is the guidance for all souls, and it quickly tries to find a remedy that is best for a soul in all situations.

Dr. Ronda's reflection:

A mentor of mine always ends any plea for advice with "pray, pray, pray." And, indeed, Padre Pio famously taught: "pray, don't worry."

For you:

Every time you feel worried, pray right away until you feel more peaceful.

Your thoughts or experiences:

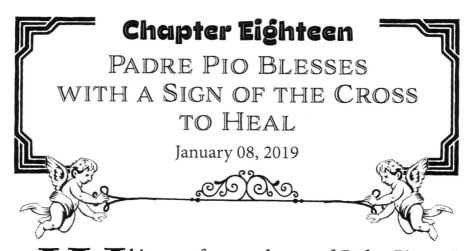

Chapter Eighteen

PADRE PIO BLESSES WITH A SIGN OF THE CROSS TO HEAL

January 08, 2019

Waking up from a dream of Padre Pio at 5 A.M. is something I did not expect this morning. Padre Pio came to me in a dream, and I knew my situation with my husband would be taken care of by God. Padre Pio had been reaching out to me in previous dreams and is the one of the main reasons. I will now proceed to tell you about the dream.

An emergency had occurred the night before, where my husband, Doug had a brain bleed. His second brain surgery was performed to keep his brain from internal bleeding and swelling. The second brain surgery occurred nine months after his first brain surgery which had taken place as stated as to several months earlier or to be precise March 30, 2018.

After this second brain surgery in 2019, he was placed into the Intensive Care Unit (ICU). It was a rough night!

There was still swelling in the brain and his blood pressure drop dramatically in the ICU. So, his monitoring by a nurse was consistent throughout the night. She sat in front of a glass window hardly leaving this area as she monitored and charted his vitals. She told me, "His blood pressure is very low but we will continue to monitor it. "You need to go home and get some rest, we will call you immediately if you are needed here." I put all my faith in God and decided to go home to shower and get some sleep if it was even possible.

I was so tired when I arrived at home, but I started to pray the rosary in my bed. I fell asleep and woke up with the rosary in my hand at 5 A.M. The dream is amazing! I could not believe what I had just dreamt but it was a certainty to me that all would be just fine. Let me take you into the dream journey of direct contact with a saint in a dream.

This is the dream…I was standing on a concrete sidewalk and noticed a man gently walking towards me from a distance with two men in perfect union (one on each side of him). They did not speak to me but accompanied the saint without missing a single step and walked perfectly along his side as they were dressed in white.

It was the Saint Padre Pio, who was wearing an unwrinkled brown cloak. He did have a beard. He finally stopped walking and stood about one to two feet away from me making eye contact, while extending and raising his right hand. He made a huge 'Sign of the Cross' very slowly and blessed me very slowly. I just stood numb. It was a beautiful blessing!

Then something made me turn around all the sudden. It was a beautiful statue of the Blessed Mother Mary, crying with tears running down her cheeks. I looked down and saw plenty of beautiful tall pale pink roses at her feet on the ground. The tall pale pink roses were all beautifully intact as they laid on the floor next to her. So, I quickly turned around and saw the saint with his two companions (next to him on each side) walking slowly away in unison.

I woke up from the dream! I quickly looked at my clock, as is customary after I dream this way. It was now 5 A.M. This is where comprehension and understanding took place immediately as I realized the saint came to bless me and that he was sent by a loving mother, our Blessed Mother, to assure me that all would be all right with my husband's health. The tall pale pink roses represent a mother's love and peace.

So, I quickly got up and started my morning routine with great peace before heading to the hospital to see my husband. I arrived at the hospital to visit my husband in the ICU to find out he dramatically improved, with now a normal blood pressure, and with swelling subsiding from his brain. Doug was out of the hospital in a couple of days. Up to now, he has no deficiencies and no medications with MRI scans of the brain showing up as normal. I am so grateful and thankful to God!

So, saints do pray and intercede to God for us when we need the prayers. Never give up on praying or on the power of prayer. Pray to our friends in heaven, the saints for intercession on all causes for they will gladly go to the Almighty in petition for our crosses in life. This is a moment of God's love radiating in our realm through something simple and humble, as a dream. Thanking God for everything, always!

Dr. Ronda's reflection:

I once had a miraculous healing of awful discomfort in the jaw area. A priest prayed over me and the sensation of two years of misery went away.

For you:

What do you need healing for?

Your thoughts or experiences:

141

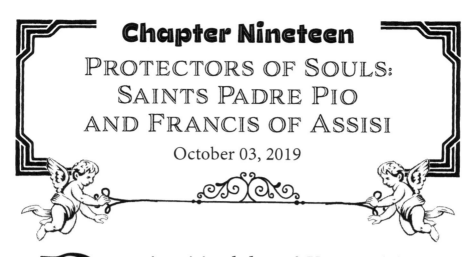

Chapter Nineteen

PROTECTORS OF SOULS:
SAINTS PADRE PIO
AND FRANCIS OF ASSISI

October 03, 2019

Dramatic spiritual dream! Upon arriving at a particular home to visit, the back door was open. It being early dawn and dressed in white, I was there for a particular reason, but sincere doubt soon came over me as to who was within the visiting home, since the back door was open for anyone to enter.

I decided to go to the front door of the house and found it to be opened ajar or slightly opened but not widely opened; yet, not closed or a locked front door. Now, I was inside the home through its front door, and I saw an envelope. Something dramatic was inside the envelope. I found the number of the beast written, all three numbers clearly and boldly written out, and placed within the envelope. Evil had identified itself within the dream!

I proceeded to walk within the home and entered a bedroom. I was now in a battle and in trouble. Yes, it was an evil battle. My emotions in the dream were fear and pain. I was very scarred and felt pain as my hand felt scratched. It felt like a sharp bristle brush scraping my hand. I was being attacked by an invisible evil entity and it did not want me within this home.

What happens next is amazing! All of the sudden, a short man, dressed in a Capuchin Friar brown tunic with a white cord tied around his waist and rosary beads, grabbed my hand. I was able to identify him because his head is not covered, so I saw him clearly in my dream. He had a white beard with white hair. His demeanor was of urgency. He would not let go of my hand. I looked up and it was Saint Padre Pio.

He grabbed the hand I had been scratched on and tightly enclosed it with his hand, never letting go and guiding me out of the home. We both walked side by side while he held my hand until he got me out of the home and outside to the front yard of the home. He turned around and disappeared from the premises.

So, as usual I woke up my husband to tell him of the dream. Doug told me, "Tomorrow is the Feast Day of St. Francis of Assisi." St. Francis died on October 03, 1226, and my dream took place October 03, 2019. However, St. Francis Feast Day would be the next day October 04th.

St. Francis of Assisi he had once kissed the hand of a leper and felt he had to kiss the hand because God was testing him. St. Francis of Assisi did not fail God. One night the Pope dreamed of St. Francis needing help to rebuild the church. He was to receive St. Francis to communicate with him.

Later, St. Francis established a religious order and known throughout the world. St. Francis of Assisi was Padre Pio's favorite person since Padre Pio was a Capuchin of the order of St. Francis of Assisi.

I realized that in my dream the saint was protecting me from a demonic entity, by personally escorting me out of the evil home into a safe environment. Once his mission of getting me safely out of the home in my dream, the Capuchin

Friar disappeared from my dream. Saint Francis of Assisi and Saint Padre Pio pray for all souls and guide all souls to the way of God.

Dr. Ronda's reflection:

Without having mystical visions as Alicia has them, we very often are disturbed by evil thoughts. It helps me to pray immediately to my favorite saints and my guardian angel.

For you:

Do you rebuke evil thoughts? A simple prayer is this one: I rebuke the spirit of ___ (anxiety or hatred, or melancholy...) Jesus, take it away."

Your thoughts or experiences:

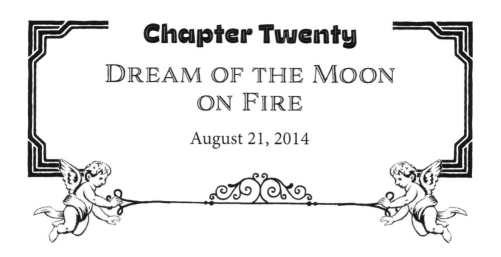

Chapter Twenty

DREAM OF THE MOON ON FIRE

August 21, 2014

Unfortunately, I dreamed this morning of a full red moon on complete fire in the sky and moving throughout the skies. There in the middle of all this stood people from all different nationalities and social economic groups watching the large moon on fire in the middle of the street. The rest of the area was dark. If there is any meaning to this dream, what could it mean?

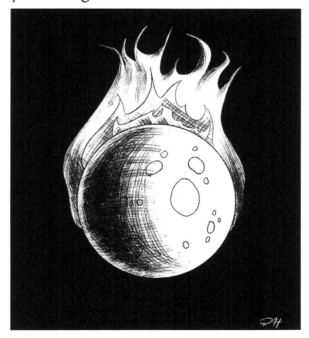

Dr. Ronda's reflection:

At the Marian apparition site in Medjugorje I saw in 1989 the sun spinning and then becoming a huge white ball, throbbing, surrounded by light and a purple sky. It seemed to me to be a symbol of the promised 'new heaven and a new earth.'

For you:

Have you ever seen such a vision? If not, you might look at a film about Fatima and see the miracle of the sun.

Your thoughts or experiences:

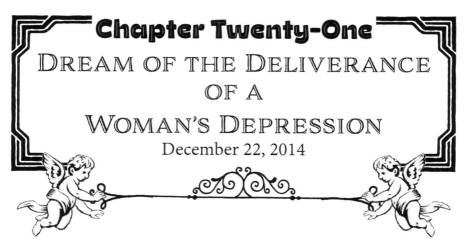

Chapter Twenty-One
DREAM OF THE DELIVERANCE OF A WOMAN'S DEPRESSION
December 22, 2014

(Since this is actual person I am writing about, for the purpose of privacy, I will use the name 'Jane'.)

Jane is an actual person I know who lives in a three-bedroom home with no hot water, no air conditioning and is infested with termites.

Jane became very depressed over her poor health and living conditions. She felt helpless over her life situation. The emotional loss of her mother whom she treasured and lived with for so many years became an added burden to her well-being both physically and psychologically. They were very close. She always cried about the great loss of her cherished mother.

One day I told Jane it was time for a new change in her life. She did not see it or understand how that would even happen.

So, I inquired about help for Jane by completing all the necessary paperwork to demolish her old home and get a new home through a grant. In addition, I made sure she would keep and save her money for new household items such as a new range over the period of two years. The purpose of her saving small amounts of money over a period was to alleviate financial stress since she had limited amount of money to make large purchases at a whim. These items would now be delivered paid in full to her home. The funniest and hilarious thing we laughed about all the time is my new title given to me by Jane, 'Chief Executive Financial Officer.'

It was two days in a row of nonstop working with Jane from December 22 - 23, 2014 from the early morning hours until 9 P.M. The extremely busy two days with Jane were to make sure all her storage items, new curtains, furniture would be moved into her new home.

Jane now has a new home! It was ready for her to move into it on the third day before Christmas. The new home was much smaller than the old, demolished home, but it was now beautifully decorated with furniture. It had all the necessities of air conditioning and heat for her own comfort. Jane received her keys on December 22, 2014. She was now ecstatically happy!

After a couple of days, I had the following dream and called Jane to tell her about it. She told me she understood the dream and it made perfect sense to her.

In the dream, I was standing in Jane's front yard dressed in white. I looked all around me in a three hundred sixty-degree view. I saw Jane's neighbors sitting in a picnic table chatting next door. Suddenly, I turned around and saw Jane in the middle of the street with water up to her knees facing her home. I made a turn again and saw wild animals heading towards her yard. I saw a wolf and four cubs looking from behind the other neighbor's chain link fence into her yard. The wolf was standing there looking into the yard, but the cubs were spilling into her yard through the fence.

Next, I turned again and saw a skinny fast brown Jaguar running down her sidewalk to the end of her street. Things start to happen when a woman in the neighbor's picnic area appeared within the dream. The women scared the animal away. But there was a black panther walking towards Jane's house and the woman once again lured the animal away. This time I turn towards Jane's house and looked underneath the house to see a puddle of water and within the reflection I saw a black panther's paw reflecting off the puddle of water walking underneath the house. So, I yelled to the woman warning her about the panther lurking under Jane's home.

The woman without hesitation, quickly walked around Jane's house, and stood directly in front of the home where the panther was lurking. The woman had light brown hair and her age was in the thirty's. She wore a beautiful fall dress. She gently motioned the panther to come out from the home. She patted him gently on the face and nose. Then the woman started pulling on two thick heavy chains about thirty feet long and three inches thick and wrapped it around the black panther's neck. Without any force, she gently pulled the black panther out from underneath Jane's house. The panther was obedient to the woman and came out slowly. The black panther pulled by the woman with the heavy chains and gently strolled down the driveway and out the gates of Jane's front property.

The woman in the dream was Jane's deceased mother. She died in her late seventy's but in my dream her mother's age was around the thirty's. The woman was young and perfectly happy in my dream.

I woke up and told my husband the dream. I wrote the dream into my journal. Next, I called Jane to tell her the dream.

Jane told me, "The woman you were dreaming was my mother and guardian angel," and "She was the angel assisting in taking the chains of depression away and out of the gates of the home."

There was so much symbolism in this dream of a large black panther, a wolf with four cubs, a jaguar, puddles of reflecting water and the deceased young mother. Wow! What a way to dream.

Dr. Ronda's reflection:

I am more delighted and amazed at Alicia's huge donation of time to help "Jane" than by the dream!

Even though I have never undertaken such a mission, I do give a lot to the poor. May I one day see them in our home in heaven.

For you:

Do you suffer from depression? Are there ways you can seek help for depressing aspects of your life?

Your thoughts and reflection:

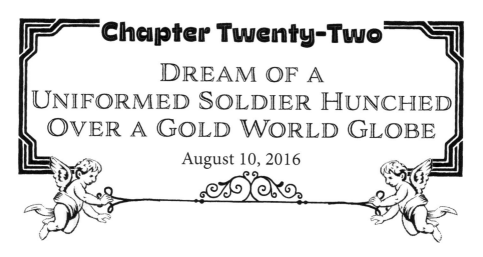

Chapter Twenty-Two

DREAM OF A UNIFORMED SOLDIER HUNCHED OVER A GOLD WORLD GLOBE

August 10, 2016

A weird and unusual dream. I freaked out because not even my husband could interpret the dream for me. He did not understand the dream.

In the dream, I was in a neat clean hospital and was to be seen for a cold. I took the chart from a nurse who told me, "Go to the back and you will be seen."

I proceeded to walk towards the back. As I walked out through the door, I saw a large golden oblong sphere (world). It was almost round, but not totally round. I could not avoid passing it because it was in front of me, as I passed the door heading towards the back. The golden sphere or world was not solid, it had links throughout it (openings). I saw a soldier dressed in his military uniform with his helmet and boots hunched over this golden world (not solid but open with links). The helmet was intact and stayed on the solider without falling off him, even though he was hunched over the world. His upper extremities were facing down on the golden world, so I was unable to view the face. His boots are hanging by the strap at the lower part of the golden globe.

I stood speechless watching the soldier hunched over the world. As I continue to look around, I saw rooms with several gurneys with people on them. I kept walking on the walking. On the way I saw another room with lots of gurneys and people getting medical attention. It was a clean place with clean floors. I did not see any blood just a lot of sick people. However, what freaked me out in my dream was the non-mobile hunched over soldier with his helmet not falling off with the boots strapped on the bottom of the golden world (sphere).

A reader of these dreams thinks it could have been a symbol of how soldiers protect the world. I agree!

Dr. Ronda's reflection:

I like to commend all police and soldiers for risking their lives protecting us.

For you:

Who do you thank for protection?

Your thoughts or experiences:

Chapter Twenty-Three
DREAM OF MARY IN A GAZEBO
August 14, 2016

I dreamt of being within a large boat. The huge waves of water were landing on the boat. The dangerous and treacherous waves are beating on the boat. It was a scary moment, but I was able to get off the boat to walk away to safety.

However, where I was standing, I saw water seeping through the cracks of the concrete on the ground. The water was rising slowly from the ground.

I continued to walk to a park that had plants and a gazebo, with the Blessed Mother Mary within the gazebo. I stood in front of the gazebo and looked at the Blessed Mother who was crying profusely. I think this is where all the water was coming from, and it was her tears spilling onto the ground! She was crying with both beautiful hands covering her face. She cried gracefully and continuously without stopping.

I spoke to her saying, "Do not cry, LET IT BE! We will pray harder."

She was never consoled and continued crying non-stop in my dream with both her hands never leaving her face.

Dr. Ronda's reflection:

In the Middle Ages Catholics let their tears enter vails. They considered them precious signs of a soft heart. To be hard hearted is a sign of being cold, without love! The Danish Lutheran theologian, Kierkegaard, once wrote that the sins of others should cause us not to gossip, but to weep!

For You:

Try to sigh, if not cry, for your own sins and those of others.

Your thoughts or experiences:

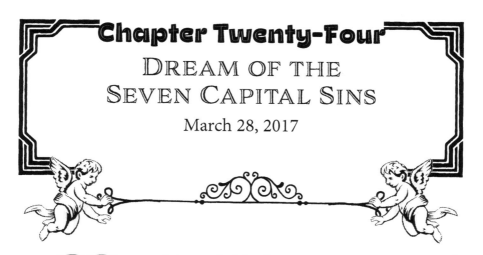

Chapter Twenty-Four
DREAM OF THE SEVEN CAPITAL SINS
March 28, 2017

My writing of this dream is not meant to offend or judge any person or situation. It is not based on any personal opinions, but it is a revealing dream of many sins becoming human beings with faulty mouths (cursing) and refusal to acknowledge the name, Jesus. In other words, these sins become human or better yet to describe them more accurately, demons. Demons lie and never will reveal a 'truth' to any person for they are seeking souls to torment in the fire of Hell. They bring doubt to a person and false assurances of a person's sin abilities to make sure they are never extinguished with a lid on them. We are never to speak to an evil entity for they will never reveal a truth but mislead you. However, in this dream I yell back at them and threaten them with the name of Jesus, who they could never pronounce at all. They avoid mentioning the name above all names both on earth and below, which is the name, 'Jesus.'

Here is a dream I had at exactly midnight.

I saw four apartment rooms painted in green. The rooms were all cubed and adjacent to each other, so the other three rooms all held some of the seven capital sins, which became vivid and alive to me in this dream.

What did I see? It was the seven capital sins. Lust was prominent in each of the rooms, but each room held its own theme. But all seven other capital sins were present in each room as follows: Envy, Pride, Greed, Gluttony, Anger, Lust and Sloth and revealed themselves so badly that they became human beings in each room.

Each room had a theme of a capital sin. I do not wish to explain exactly what I saw in my dream because it is too much.

However, I will mention the following:

In the first room, I saw the sin of same sex activity relationships going on in the first room.   For there were many people in this room, an overpopulated room.

In the second room, I saw the sin of adultery between a man and a woman. For there was a beautiful shiny golden band (sacrament of marriage) laying on the night stand next to the adulterous bed of the man and woman.

In the third room, I saw the sin of sex among many people in the last room. For there were multiple genders of people lacking respect for one another.

In my dream I could clearly see all three bedrooms adjacent before me and all the activities in each room occurring at the same time, as I stood looking from the empty fourth room able to view all people (capital sins) and actions in the other rooms. But to me, they are revealing or taunting demons whose mission is to torment a people by lashing out their evil desires upon every man which are the capital sins that offend the Sacred Heart of Jesus.

Dressed in white standing before me are three rooms. Simultaneously, I can view all of these three rooms at the same time. It is like looking through a clear glass, but there was none. In other words, there was no walls inside between me and the three rooms. There are no doors or walls that blocked my witnessing of these rooms. It was transparent to my eyes. Each room held a serious capital sin that destroyed the Heart of the Sacred Heart of Jesus. Each room was vivid and held a serious sin, so serious that in my dream I could no longer stand it and finally physically stepped into the last room of the sin of sex among many people.

In anger, I yelled to the people in this room and commanded the following, "What have you done with the Sacred Heart image?" "Where is it?" "Give it to me NOW!"

In my dream, the multiple people in the third room having sex with multiple people and feasting on food replied to me, "We do not know what you are talking about" and continued saying, "We have never seen your Sacred Heart." They did not say the name Jesus.

I yelled even louder at them and demanded, "You better find it NOW and give it to me! NOW!"

As they did not cooperate with me, they stood there looking at me, I took it upon myself and started searching throughout the room. I searched under the linens and covers. I went through all the items throughout the room.

I finally found it!

They had torn it apart and destroyed it by crumbling the frame of the Sacred Heart image. I brought the torn and crumbled frame up to my chest of the Sacred Heart image to wail out loud.

I woke up and told my husband. I had a difficult day forgetting this dream. I can't help dreaming this way.

I am not judging anyone! It is simply a horrible dream. I just want to share how vivid my dreams seem at times. It helps to write and speak about them.

After reflecting on this dream for some time, I realize the Sacred Heart of Jesus novenas, prayers, images, chaplets are a threat to the atrocities of the capital sins brought onto many by evil or venomous entities. So, I recommend a blessed Sacred Heart image in your own bedroom or children's rooms. Evil cannot stand the beautiful Sacred Heart of Jesus image; it is too much for demons. They can never measure up to Jesus's beautiful face and heart.

To summarize the dream, it was a dream of major sins of same sex sexual activity, adultery, orgies with multiples sins in these cubed (square) small green apartment rooms. I image green apartments to be interpreted as the main symbolism to the sin of pride which leads to the sin of greed, therefore producing many other capital sins. It was an awful dream!

Dr. Ronda's reflection:

After the Second Vatican Council, some Catholic teachers and preachers tried to minimize the evil of sexual sins. Some wanted Catholics falling into sin not to despair and leave the Church. Some themselves had become frequent in such sins. God created the sexual urge to lead to marriages, with a nest for the newborns, not for pleasure unrelated to our deep vocations.

For you:

You might go to the Catechism of the Catholic Church and read about sexuality to refresh your understanding of the beauty of good, moral sex versus sin.

Your thoughts or Experiences:

Chapter Twenty-Five

DREAM OF THE TREE OF LIFE

June 01, 2017

It is early morning Thursday, the Seventh and last week of Easter 2017 with all in my household still sleeping. I awoke from a beautiful dream and entitled it, The Tree of Life. Upon awaking, I quickly pulled out my notebook and began drawing my dream on notebook paper, it looks like a bunch of scribble. At that time, my wish was to be a talented artist so I could draw it beautifully; however, I am not a talented artist. I can only describe the dream with the hope of you capturing its beauty.

I was wearing a simple white gown which covered my arms up to the wrists. The dress flowed freely on the grass as I walked in the surrounding evergreen grass as underneath the tree.

It was mesmerizing to find myself standing underneath an extremely beautiful large tree. The tall tree took my breath as I turned every way looking up at the tree to see the surroundings of the beauty of this large evergreen tree.

It was a tall evergreen tree with a huge trunk and large sturdy roots in the ground. The tree had extended sheltering evergreen and plentiful leaves on its branches. I say evergreen leaves on the branches, but the color was beyond the evergreen color that we see here on earth. It was beyond any greens I have seen anywhere else, for it was amazing!

I stood underneath this beautiful tree and looking up to admire the beautiful tree. The tree being so extremely tall made me look exceedingly small by comparison. The branches hovered about twenty feet above my head. Everything surrounding the tree was a beautiful green color. This green cannot be fully described as green. It was a mixture of a deep green combined with a mixture of emerald, green on the tree's branches. It is difficult to interpret the color. However, it is an extremely beautiful green!

I could not help admiring the beautiful tree. I take notice immediately of the tree having crystal-clear crisp water freely flowing out of it into a nearby crystal stream of flowing water. It was crystal-clear like fine crystal; except I would say the fine crystal we see is about twenty percent of what the crystal water may be compared to as it flows out of that dream tree.

Get this! The tree had pure silver font open taps attached to it. The pure silver taps are widely opened for the clear water to freely flow out of the beautiful tree. The taps looked like something you see in a church or a drink dispenser. The taps were not only silver, but of purest fine silver. In other words, the pure fine silver taps are attached to different areas of the tree (one tap was way above my head) so the water could rush out of the tree through the taps into a small crystal-clear stream near the tree. The water that came out of the bark of the tree overflowed freely into the ground. It then formed different routes of passages of water going out into other areas of the ground.

I awoke realizing I just dreamed of the 'Tree of Life.' Upon awaking I quickly wrote the dream down and sought an interpretation in confession by a priest. The priest who heard my confession told me, "It is a good dream and there is nothing wrong with dreaming about God. In the Bible, the tree signifies God since he is the tree of life." Amazing! I thought God pours out his blessing and we gather graces in form of blessed water to be baptized and anointing of oils. All of these are gifts from God onto every living being. The gift of life and the sacraments of the church are the gifts by God to all. So, I understood the tree found in the Bible to be very sacred and it signifies God.

I decided to look up the tree of life in the Bible it is mentioned in both Genesis 3:24 and Revelations 22. This is what I read in Genesis 3:24, "So he drove out the man; and he placed at the east of the garden of Eden Cherubim, and a flaming sword and turned every way, to keep the way of the tree of life." I went further on to read the scriptures of Revelations 22, regarding the Tree of Life, I read the following:

"Then the angel showed me the river of life, rising from the throne of God and of the Lamb and flowing crystal-clear. Down the middle of the city street, on either bank of the river were the tree of life, which bear twelve crops of fruit in a year, one in each month, and the leaves of which are the cure for the nations. The curse of destruction will be abolished. The throne of God and of the Lamb will be in the city; his servants will worship him, they will see him face to face, and his name will be written on their foreheads. And night will be abolished; they will not need lamp-light or sunlight, because the Lord God will be shining on them. They will reign for ever and ever. The angel said to me, 'All that you have written is sure and will come true: the Lord God who inspires the prophets has sent his angel to reveal to his servants what is soon to take place. I am coming soon!' Blessed are those who keep the prophetic message of this book. I, John, am the one who heard and saw these things. When I had heard and seen them all, I knelt at the feet of the angel who had shown them to me, to worship him; but he said, 'Do no such thing: I am your fellow-servant and the fellow-servant of your brothers the prophets and those who keep the message of this book. God alone you must worship.' This, too, he said to me, 'Do not keep the prophecies in this book a secret, because the Time is close. Meanwhile let the sinner continue sinning, and the unclean continue to be unclean; let the upright continue in his uprightness, and those who are holy continue to be holy. Look, I am coming soon, and my reward is with me, to repay everyone as their deeds deserve. I am the Alpha and the Omega, the First and the Last, the Beginning and the End. Blessed are those who will have washed their robes clean, so that they will have the right to feed on the tree of life and can come through the gates into the city. Others must stay outside: dogs, fortune-tellers, and the sexually immoral, murderers, idolaters, and everyone of false speech and false life.' I, Jesus, have sent my angel to attest these things to you for the sake of the churches. I am the sprig from the root of David and the bright star of the morning. The Spirit and the Bride say, 'Come!' Let everyone who listens answer, 'Come!' Then let all who are thirsty come: all who want it may have the water of life, and have it free. This is my solemn attestation to all who hear the prophecies in this book: if anyone adds anything to them, God will add to him every plague mentioned in the book; if anyone cuts anything out of the prophecies in this book, God will cut off his share of the tree of life and of the holy city, which are described in the book. The one who attests these things says: I am indeed coming soon. Amen; come, Lord Jesus. May the grace of the Lord Jesus be with you all. Amen" (Douay-Rheims New Testament, Apoc. 22)

Dr. Ronda's reflection:

I love every word of this prophecy except the word "soon." How ambiguous is the word "soon!" Is it likely St. John thought soon meant more than two thousand years hence?

Nonetheless in our times so full of evil and suffering how good it is to believe in this predicted future and work toward it in faith.

For you:

Read this dream and citation slowly savoring it.

Your thoughts or experiences:

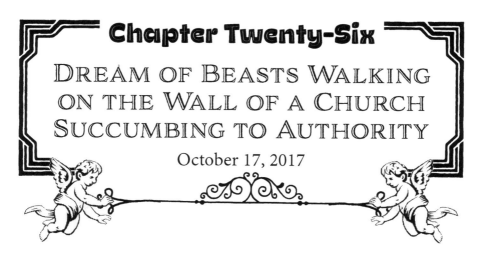

Chapter Twenty-Six

DREAM OF BEASTS WALKING ON THE WALL OF A CHURCH SUCCUMBING TO AUTHORITY

October 17, 2017

In this dream, it was early morning as I drove a white vehicle, which in real life I do not own a white vehicle. I was on the way to pick up my son from school in this white vehicle and managed to get through heavy traffic without problems. I exit the expressway by yielding and proceed to a stop sign.

I was now turning into a side street. It was no longer early morning, but late evening. I stopped my vehicle in front of a church.

I looked to my right side to see a church building, but I could no longer drive the vehicle. I was witnessing a dark moment on the brick wall of a church. Therefore, I placed my vehicle on park in front of the building. I wanted to make sense of what I was viewing on the brick walls of the church.

I saw a seven to eight-foot-long and about three to four feet wide large black beast (large type of a wild cat-like) animal. For reference in this dream, I will interchangeably refer to the animal as a black beast.

I could not believe it! So, I parked my vehicle in front of this church building. There it was! An exceptionally large black beast gently strolling on all his four legs on the outdoor brick wall of the church building.

Then next to this black beast, I notice another animal, just like it, also walking the brick wall of the Church along with the other wild beast. Again, both are huge animals walking on all their four legs on the brick wall of the church from top to the bottom. I stayed inside the vehicle to view them walk on the brick wall of the church. They were extremely large beast (cat-like) animals or panthers, so huge and so was their purpose on the grounds of the church.

What is so unusual in this dream is that the animals are walking on the brick wall of the church. Separately, these large animals were several feet apart, as they alternate walking up and down on the wall from top to the bottom without pausing but seem to be trying to inscribe something on the wall.

Both animals were trying to inscribe something on the outside wall of the church. They are working hard in inscribing something on the church walls, but I did not bother to read what it was because I was so terrified in viewing all the activity on the church walls.

As I was viewing the inscribing on the wall, for I was about to try to read it, my vehicle had a glitch. My headlights went off completely on their own. I was now in complete darkness and unable to see anything at all.

So, I took a risk and decided to drive the vehicle down the street slowly without any headlights in hopes of finding someone to tell what was happening down the street at the church.

In the dream, a glimpse of hope showed up as I saw two people approaching down the road and driving slowly by me. I yelled out to them, "Help! There is something strange happening at the church down the street."

So, I began to follow their vehicle back to the church. Since everything was so dark, they drew out flashlights. They became witnesses from their vehicle of these two animals walking on all their fours on the church walls. They used flashlights because all the grounds of the church were in total darkness. They are stunned in the dream.

Then the dream changed once again for I then witnessed one of these large wild animals calmly walking just like a predator through some high grassy area, as I stood in the grassy area to view what the animal was prowling after, but it could not see me standing there watching it prowl through the high grassy area.

The dream took a change again, I was now inside and sitting down within the building of the church. As, I sat down to view what is happening I saw the following: one of the animals strolled a couple of feet from me and passed me, for it could not see me sitting within the church. An extremely large animal!

To me what happened next is an act of obedience to God and church authority. This is how I interpret this next scenario. As the animal strolled by me, I am representing the average person or having a strong faith, took out a cross from inside my blouse. It walked past me and did not stop upon the making of the sign of the cross. Faith matters in all things!

Now, the dream changes again I saw a calm, peaceful and tranquil priest dressed in white sitting on a large chair in the center of the large room. I am viewing this at a distance, where the priest or the beasts could not see me. The beast walked a short distance in front of the priest sitting on his chair dressed in white. The large beast walked by the priest and walked to the far opposite right side of the room to flop

175

its body, as it laid down like a bear. It's huge body just laid down and its head placed on the floor resting on its chin. It had a face of close resemblance to a bear with eyes that did not close at all. It lay down on the floor with its eyes wide open!

Now, suddenly there was a third animal just like the previous two animals. It did all the same motions as the previous animals, such as passing the priest on the chair and laying down with its eyes open as it rested its chin on the floor. It looked as if their entire bodies flopped in obedience on the floor with the chins resting on the floor and their eyes wide open.

There were several animals in an orderly fashion one at a time and minutes apart as they continued to walk by the priest to lie down in the position describe above. I lost count but there must have been seven, twelve or thirteen of them. I do not know the exact number; it was quite a lot of them. They all lined up and apart from one another on their bellies with their chins touching the floor and their eyes wide open. They slept this way without movement. Now, as I see them lying still without movement, I noticed some of the color of the large cats range from black and others were brown. I quickly woke up!

I interpret the dream as the beast are obedient to the Cross and the making of the sign of the cross, which is a witness to a strong faith. Now, since I was witnessing all of this from behind and at a slight distance from the priest dressed in all white sitting on a large chair, I assumed all these animals (beast) became obedient towards authority, as the priest dressed in white on a large chair represented the authority of the church.

The beast were merely creatures, which had to succumb

to supreme authority, the church. Even though they scurried their way around the church, they had no authority before the priest on the chair. In the end, the beast was without authority and motionless because it saw the strong faith of Christianity in the making of the Cross before their own bodies which put their souls to sleep with their eyes wide open.

Dr. Ronda's reflection:

I loved this dream because of the crisis in the church with some Catholics of all vocations dissenting about church teaching. May higher authorities win their assent!

For you:

What is your attitude toward dissent?

Your thoughts and experiences:

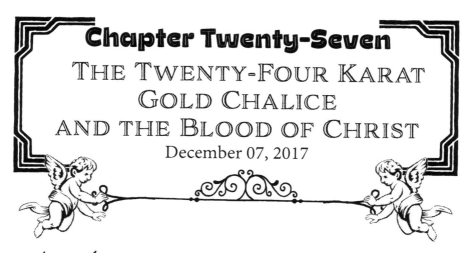

Chapter Twenty-Seven

THE TWENTY-FOUR KARAT GOLD CHALICE AND THE BLOOD OF CHRIST

December 07, 2017

he dream this morning is so unusual with lots of symbolism. Upon waking up, I questioned how is it I dream this way?

Inside a large building with no windows are plenty of people filling up the rows of seats. It looked like an auditorium. It seemed like an event would be starting soon and people were getting situated around this large place in their seats. It seemed as if a large Mass would be taking place.

I now see myself kneeling and confessing before a holy priest who was standing in front of the altar but behind the altar railings just slightly to the left side of it. He was behind the altar railing and listening to my confession. I must admit every time I go to confession, I ramble on about how I love God and talk a little before confessing, so in my dream I did the same.

The holy priest stood there with his both hands folded, as in prayer, to listen. He moved his head to acknowledge listening to my confession. He was dressed in all white. He was elder holy man with extremely snow-white hair and beard. He had a real gold rope belt around his waist. He looked extremely holy. The holy priest stood feet away while listening to my confession but never came too close to me for he was behind the altar rail.

I will call the priest a 'Holy Priest' in my dream from now on. The 'Holy Priest' behind the altar rail turned around to go behind the altar that was in front of me as I knelt. Everything shined! For it was real gold except his clothing which was super snow white with his matching snow-white hair. He started the Mass. He had a shiny real twenty-four gold large golden chalice at the altar. I watched him say Mass in amazement, as I knelt in front of the railing.

This is where it gets strange. The holy priest gave me from his hands the twenty-four-karat gold large golden chalice. I stood up to take the chalice from him. I was directed to transport this chalice from this holy priest to another church or area. So, taking the gold chalice in my hand I drank some of the precious blood.

I proceeded to walk with the precious blood in the gold chalice out of the church into what look like an exceedingly long hallway. As, I walked down this long hallway, I saw all doors wide open in the area or rooms within parts this building.

I knew I was to walk in one area with the precious blood in the golden chalice. I glanced into this large auditorium room to see the following: a priest sitting with their books (green books) and nuns sitting towards the front. They were all kneeling and praying. They were sitting on the left side of the pews. Now, I noticed on the right side of the pews where the ordinary people were kneeling and praying. They were all kneeling and praying looking towards the front.

As I looked to the front, I saw huge rock or bolder (guessing over twenty to thirty feet high) at the front of all these pews. On this huge rock were two girls dressed in long white gowns with short hair, between twelve and fourteen years old. They were standing on the top of rock, as they anxiously awaited the arrival of the precious blood. One of girls had a purifier on her arm. The two young girls had huge radiating smiles on their faces. They were so happy and beaming!

I entered the area with the golden chalice filled with the precious blood of Jesus carrying it in my hands. I walked all the way to the front of the huge boulder or rock. Easily, I climbed the rock while holding the large golden chalice with both hands and reached the top of the rock where the two smiling beaming girls were awaiting the chalice. It was a huge rock and looked difficult to climb, but I had no problem. I keep both hands on the chalice until I finally reached the top of the rock.

When I reached the top of the rock. I gave the golden chalice to one the young girls dressed in white. She took the chalice and looked inside of it and with a large smile said, "You did not drink it all" and gave it back to me.

So, I looked inside the chalice and noticed the inside of the chalice looked like the rock or boulder I and the two girls were standing on. I find three or four drops still inside the chalice.

I took the chalice from her hands and tilted my head back to drink the final drops of the precious blood of Jesus until the chalice was all empty. Upon drinking all the precious blood, I gave the chalice back to the young girl on the rock. She looked inside the chalice once again and said with a large happy smile, "Thank you" and took the chalice I brought to her. The other young girl standing next to her dressed in a white robe handed her the church purifier linen. The young girl started to clean the chalice very well from inside and around the rim. I turned around and easily climbed down the huge rock without any trouble.

As, I started walking out of the area, the religious people on the left were still kneeling and praying.

However, the people on the right that were kneeling and praying, stood up as I was walking out and complained from across the room, "We have been praying so hard, but we seem not to accomplish anything! There are still problems! There are earthquakes, fires and things still going bad!"

I kept walking but yelled right back, "Just keep praying and pray harder! Do not stop praying!" I hastily proceeded to walk out for I did not want to hear them complain. As I turn to look back, the people complaining on the right were still talking and chatting among themselves, so I shut all the doors so they would be quiet as I left the area.

Then I proceeded back to the original area I came from to see another Mass still going on by the holy priest.

I woke up to cry for I realized in my dream: I transported the chalice with the precious blood from one church to another church, I had confession prior to transporting the chalice from one church to another church and I had delivered the golden chalice to two angelic angels on the highest rock before all types of people in society. I am not too sure, but I think I confessed and dreamt a holy priest with extreme snow-white hair and beard with a golden belt may be a High Priest who enters the Temple of Jerusalem into the Holy of Holies once a year. The reason I say this because years later, I looked up the golden belt and it is usually a High Priest that has this vestment. I do not know… What a way to dream! Anyway, this holy priest with a golden belt around his waist in my dream heard my confession.

Dr. Ronda's reflection:

I loved when we were given the Precious Blood as part of Holy Communion at Holy Mass. Writing my comment now in 2022, we do not have this grace due to Covid precautions. I miss it.

For you:

Write your own prayer to Jesus about his precious blood.

Your thoughts and experiences:

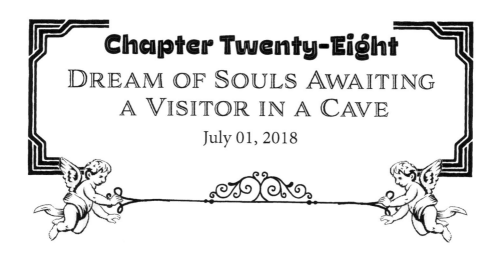

Chapter Twenty-Eight
DREAM OF SOULS AWAITING A VISITOR IN A CAVE
July 01, 2018

This dream is about a small cave with waiting souls. The small cave had long concrete benches attached to its concrete walls and its floors made of the same stone. The cave housed an unusual number of souls. The poor souls sat on the concrete benches on both sides of this cave. The cave was shaped in a semi-circular with openings at the end of this short circular area.

So, the cave had two opening, one to the right side, and one to the left side. The left side did not have any obstruction at its opening for the visitor would soon be walking in through this opening. The right side of the cave was covered with a partial obstruction, so I was only able to view a partial side of this opening on the right side.

I was the only person standing up in the middle of the cave, as I watched all the souls sit patiently to the right and left side on benches in the cave. They were expecting someone to arrive for them. They are waiting for someone! The visitor will soon be walking into the left obstructed side of the cave. I was not allowed to see it walk into the left side of the cave. It seems like a holding place for souls. The right side of the cave was partially viewable for it had some slight obstruction of green plantation. However, the obstructive right side of the cave was not totally viewable to me.

The souls I saw on the bench had no faces or even bodies, so I never saw their identities but they are only silhouettes. There were shapes or bodies sitting on the concrete benches. I stood there in the cave looking around to see if there was anything familiar. But it was of no avail for, there was nothing familiar to me other than it being a cold concrete place.

The souls did not mind my presence, but just sat there patiently among themselves in their sitting area on the benches. They never spoke to anyone. I felt sorry for them.

Suddenly, a young man in his early twenties with curly short hair came over to stand next to me. The visitor who these souls had been waiting on was now approaching the cave from the right side, the obstructed area. I was not allowed to see the visitor coming for the souls. I was quickly guided out to the left side of the cave immediately by the young man, so I would not see the visitor coming for the souls. So, these souls were awaiting this visitor, but I was quickly escorted out of the cave because it stopped entering on the right side of the cave until I exited out the cave with my guide on the left side of the cave. I could not look upon the visitor coming for the souls, I was quickly guided out of the cave by the young man.

I woke up!

Dr. Ronda's reflection:

This dream seemed to me to be about souls waiting for judgment. I once prayed a novena to the angels for the soul of a family member I believed was in purgatory. It felt as the soul went to heaven after that.

For you:

Ask the Holy Spirit to show you a soul to pray for.

Your thoughts or experiences:

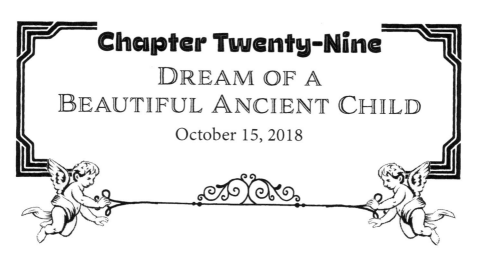

Chapter Twenty-Nine

DREAM OF A
BEAUTIFUL ANCIENT CHILD

October 15, 2018

What a way to dream!!! A beautiful ancient child! This gorgeous child lit up brilliantly and I just stood there to watch him.

Next to the child was a simple, fragile, thin, and extremely tall tree with golden branches. What was unusual about this tree is that it was all twenty-four karat GOLD. The child climbed the tree without any effort and instantly reached the top of the tree.

The ancient barefooted child dressed in a long mid-calf gown sat on the very top of the tree. I estimated the height of the tree is an extremely tall gold tree. Just image the highest tall palm tree.

The top of a tree with the child sitting up there would not be viewable to the naked eye, yet in the dream, I could see all that was going on the top of the tree. I could view the child very clearly from where I was standing.

The child sat down at the top of the tree very comfortably looking around. He was barefooted.

Then I saw an eagle. The large eagle flew around the tree. Then I saw a brilliantly lit up child. The child then changed into a round light to become a golden round light, such as the bright sun.

This bright round sun stood still at the top of the tree. I saw a large eagle fly around and land on the next branch lower than the child. The eagle finally made its landing on a golden branch.

The eagle stood still on the golden branch in joyful delight and obedience to stare at the lit-up child with obedience and admiration.

I woke up!

Dr. Ronda's reflection:

The infant Jesus? If I had seen Him, wouldn't I have been as delighted?

For you:

Picture yourself gazing at the baby Jesus.

Your thoughts or experiences:

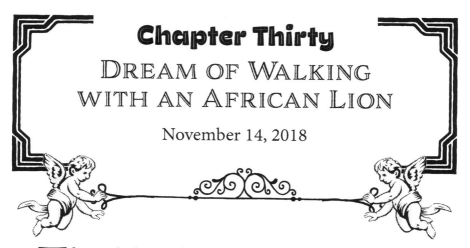

Chapter Thirty
DREAM OF WALKING WITH AN AFRICAN LION

November 14, 2018

If you believe dreams have meanings, well here is one for interpretation. Do dreams have a significant meaning? Who knows best, but here it goes and this is the dream as I woke up at 5:20 A.M. from an interesting dream of a lion.

I dreamt of an extremely large tamed African lion. It looked to weigh as much as a horse and its height was as tall

as a horse for its height was at my shoulder. The lion was over twelve feet in length.

In my dream, the large lion walked side by side with me. The large paws gently strolled the street with me just like a tamed pet's daily walk. Every step he took coincided with my steps. The large lion walked with his large paws very gently and strolled side by side, as I have mentioned earlier to you.

The people in the area watching this large animal walking side by side with me stood scared and motionless with fear as they see this large animal strolling by them.

However, I calmly walked with the lion next to my side like a tamed pet animal. Next, I directed him into a room. I showed him where his food was in the concrete room with no furniture only a large bowl for, I had food ready for the lion. Gently, the extremely large lion devoured the food I fed him.

Afterwards, gently the extremely large lion just sat down and laid down to just sit there to lovingly watch me looking at him within the same room. He was a beautiful animal. It was never aggressive or made any noise in my dream.

So, I looked up to what a lion means in Christianity, and I got this… "Jesus is the lion of the tribe of Judah. True Christians do not need a visible symbol of their faith. 2 Cor. 5:7 says they are "walking by faith, not by sight." Also, Jesus is called the Lion of Judah. (Rev 5:5) and St. Mark, who wrote one of the gospels encounters a lion. The lion encountered by St. Mark is really an angel who comes to him in form of a winged lion. I loved the dream!

Dr. Ronda's reflection:

We do not need interior visions but if God chooses to give some to us, as I believe He does with Alicia, they can enhance our faith.

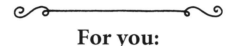

For you:

Pray for greater faith and thank God for all other graces.

Your thoughts or experiences:

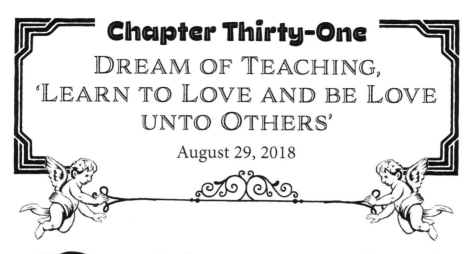

Chapter Thirty-One

DREAM OF TEACHING, 'LEARN TO LOVE AND BE LOVE UNTO OTHERS'

August 29, 2018

Dreamed of two women centered around a round table out in a public courtyard chatting among themselves. They sat there and talked badly and gossiped about others.

I was sitting at a distance quietly watching them. Suddenly, a young man around his late twenties or early thirties came and sat down at my table. He looked at me and started talking by asking me questions.

The young man in my dream looked at the two women. He asked me "What do you think those two women are doing?" I responded, "They seem to be gossiping."

The young man responded back by saying: "Yes, they seem to want to distract themselves or others from the good things in life.

So, I asked him, "Well, how does one fix this or do to avoid gossip?"

The young man in my dream turned his head towards me and said, "You cannot avoid this, but must face it. In the middle of it all, you must learn to love and be loved!" I woke up!

Dr. Ronda's reflection:

Reading the dream made me want to spend a week for starters, avoiding all gossip and only talking about necessary matters on good things.

For you:

Try doing the same.

Your thoughts or experiences:

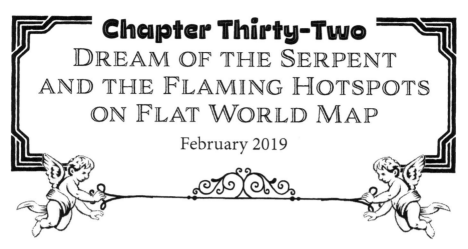

Chapter Thirty-Two
DREAM OF THE SERPENT AND THE FLAMING HOTSPOTS ON FLAT WORLD MAP
February 2019

It was a moment of total horror! I sat up in bed bewildered at such a horrible dream.

I saw a Medieval dark brick pathway and surrounding it were Italian tiles. To the right of this brick Italian pathway were several groups of open Roman arches down the pathway.

I saw a hideous thing. A large serpent he did all the actions of a man, but the face and body were all scaly with two huge very sharp curve horns on each side of its head. The serpent sat and awaited the young man who was to enter the long pathway to stand helpless before the sitting serpent's throne.

The serpent sat down within a niche on a large throne. Its body was all scaly comparable to lizard skin, but there is no skin at all because it had all scales throughout the body. It looked like a snake or lizard, taking the shape of a human. It has no nose just like a snake.

This snake talked very clearly to whoever entered the area or pathway in front of the Roman arch. The evil thing had a large curve-horseshoe of solid thick heavy bar shaped bracket brace steel around its own neck. This heavy large curve-horseshoe also looked like a bracket from a bracket from a chain link fence.

A young man entered the pathway to stand before the snake sitting on its throne. The man was wearing shorts and is barefooted. He looked helpless as he stood in this Roman long hallway or path in front of the serpent.

The young man was afraid and nervously waited for the snake to address him. Standing in front of the Roman niche, the evil snake equipped the young man with a new accessory around his neck, a solid heavy curve steel bracket pipe just like the one the serpent had on its own neck. Now the snake clearly speaks to the young man, but I could not understand what it was saying to him for it was inaudible to me.

Next, the serpent with its razor blade fingernails of several inches points to the right side of him and instructs the young man to look towards the end of a long-distance hallway. The serpent now showed the young man something of what might interest him.

It was a flat world map at the end of the hallway. The map was attached to the wall, like a framed picture of all the entire continents of the world. It had flames of fire shooting straight out of the map that was flat on the wall.

The shooting hot flames could be seen in some of the Eastern sides of North and South America. Across the Atlantic Ocean, some sporadic countries in the Mediterranean, Caspian and Red Sea areas also had hot flames shooting out of the countries on the map.

While the rest of the world also had these shooting darts of flames coming out of the map, some areas were highly visible with shooting hot flames (hotter spots) than the other areas of the world shown on the wall.

The only areas without any flames shooting out of the map were Greenland, Switzerland, and Antarctica. These three continental areas had no visible shooting fires coming from them.

I quickly woke up and sat up in my bed bewildered at such a horrible dream.

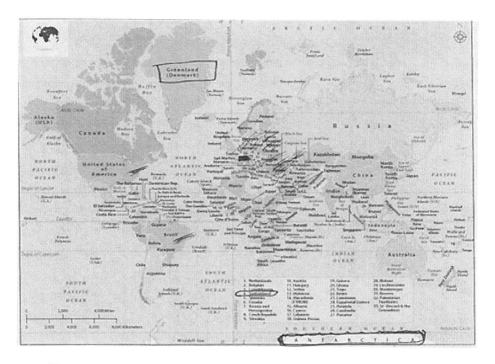

Note:

This is a map seen in this dream. The three areas boxed in green: Greenland, Antarctica and Switzerland were the only areas without no visible flames on the map in the dream. They are clear from any flames. Note to the reader, do not confuse Switzerland and Sweden. They are two different countries in two different locations.

All areas have flames coming out of the map, but there are some with a higher intense brighter flames than some other areas with light dim flames. The brightly shown flames are in red on this map as I saw it in my dream in February 2019, Dream of the Serpent and the Flaming Hotspots on Flat World Map

Dr. Ronda's reflection:

I thought the dream signified how evil the world has become. We are called to evangelize the world.

For you:

Do you think of our world as good or evil?

Your thoughts and experiences:

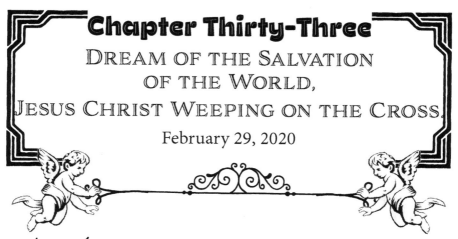

Chapter Thirty-Three

DREAM OF THE SALVATION OF THE WORLD, JESUS CHRIST WEEPING ON THE CROSS.

February 29, 2020

The time had arrived for wedding preparations **for two bridesmaids, my twin daughters,** as we three gals drove to Houston, Texas for a good friend's wedding.

In anticipation of the wedding, I knew to get some sleep; therefore, no television tonight when arriving in my hotel room. However, I was awoken from a beautiful dream in a Houston hotel. I quickly sat up in my hotel bed on a Saturday morning on February 29, 2020, at 2:45 A.M., which happened to be Leap Year Day.

It is a vivid dream of a man, Jesus Christ, The Salvation of the World crucified on the Cross.

I shall now describe HIM to you by telling you that He did not speak to me.

But He moved His legs as if they are aching in pain on the cross. There are tears streaming down His sacred face throughout the entire dream. The tears never stopped flowing from his sacred face on the cross. Never.

Jesus is incredibly beautiful as I had this vision of him.

He took the form of an actual real human being. Jesus was very tall and thin on the cross. So, he seemed tall to me on the cross like seven feet tall. However, I am not good at guessing height or measurements, so it is an estimated guess on height and on the measurements.

However, I will emphasize over again that he was not a statue, again not a statue but a real crucified man moving and crying on the cross. The cross itself is about approximately eight feet or taller.

Now, the cross is not like anything I have seen before. It was very tough thick wood. The tough wood is much larger and thicker than a wooden pole in the city. It was a rough and thick cross. It was not smooth at all.

To my surprise, Jesus' arms did not hang down slightly from the cross as depicted of Jesus in buildings or churches. Instead, Jesus's arms were straightly stretched out on this rough wooden cross and towards the bottom portion on the cross I could still see plenty of the rough wood where Jesus's arms and feet were on the cross.

One amazing thing was that there are no visible injuries to the body. Jesus did not have a crown of thrones on His sacred head. He did have a full set of hair that glowed and radiated beautifully only on the upper part of His head. Regarding His hair, a portion was viewable to me that reached to the shoulders. This portion of the hair looked soiled or drenched such as from the heat, as I was seeing some of the hair past his shoulder and the rest of the hair draped towards his back. I was unable to view the rest of His hair, as it was behind His back.

I will mention to you there was no skin color like His! It is amazing! Amazing! It is incorrect if I call it white, beige, natural or dark because none of these colors fit. The skin was perfect in color and in its clarity.

However, I did take notice of one color it is red. Our Lord has very red or irritated skin on his cheeks. More closely the description of the cheeks color was red coming from heat exhaustion or dehydration. I could clearly see this.

The closest description to me of the features of Jesus in my dream was of a Mediterranean casted deep and serious. Jesus was weeping from the beginning of the dream until He rested his head on His Sacred shoulder.

Jesus would not stop for a minute from crying. His tears flowed out of his eyes. The crystal clear tears falling or streaming from Jesus' face were clear transparent tears. The tears looked like Swarovski crystals, repeatedly falling one after the other and non-stop from His eyes.

I was so close to Him that I could even see His eyelids while on the cross. I stood right in front of Jesus on the cross about three to four feet away from Him. We locked our eyes upon one another and did not take our eyes off one another for his sacred face was in a straight position, as he was looking directly at me. We stared upon one another, like when you speak to someone close when you are looking directly into their eyes.

I could not move at all. I was incapable of doing anything such as moving, kneeling, talking and most of all, I was unable to take my eyes off HIM, because my eyes locked with His eyes. It was impossible to move the eyes even if I wanted to move them. It was impossible! I stood in front of Our Lord Jesus Christ as He was crying on the cross, as both our eyes lock upon one another.

Suddenly, I felt something behind me. I was able to quickly turn to a one hundred-eighty degrees angle to see what was behind me. This is what I saw next…

I saw people telling me to quickly turn back around to see HIM. So, I did. I quickly turned back around towards the front.

Jesus continuing to lock His dark crying eyes to mine with nonstop uncontrollable weeping. The streams of tears fell from his face one after another.

Then I saw the most astonishing thing happen next…

Jesus looked like He was in pain as He tried to move his aching legs slightly on the cross. Jesus very slowly, gently, and gracefully positioned his 'Sacred Head' from looking straight at me to now turning it very slowly, very gently, and very gracefully towards His right side. All of the sudden, Jesus gracefully let's go of all motion to rest His 'Sacred head' on His 'Sacred right shoulder.' I awoke at 2:45 A.M. in my hotel room crying from the dream.

It is a private revelation or vision in the form of a dream. I will never forget this dream. I will share with any person wishing to listen about Jesus on the Cross. Questioning myself, I concluded that perhaps it may have been a precursor or foreshadowing dream of what came a couple of weeks later.

On March 11, 2020, the WHO announced the onset of Covid 19, a devastating disease for humanity. It has shut down of churches. The disease killed many people. It was devastating!

In confession, I related the dream to a priest who told me to pray the Divine Mercy. Since I had a tough time trying to figure out the dream, I later inquired with another priest about the dream and the priest said, "It is not a dream."

So, I told the priest the following "There is nothing wrong with dreaming about the Salvation of Humanity?" He told me, "No, there is nothing wrong or bad in dreaming of Jesus on the Cross, the Savior of the World." I thank God for the beautiful dream of Jesus Christ on the Cross, the Salvation of the World and of ALL What I have written here is the truth in regards to this vision and with great love share this private revelation, vision, or dream with you. Let us all announce to the world in joy and love for we know, Jesus Christ is the Salvation of the World!

Dr. Ronda's reflection:

Some of us imagine that when many of us all over the world are afflicted by a tragic event or scourge, that God looks on from above passively. How different that if Alicia's dream was really about Covid, Jesus is suffering so deeply with us!

For you:

Did you find Jesus in the midst of your experience of Covid, yourself or in other people?

Your thoughts or experiences:

Chapter Thirty-Four

DREAM OF A WOMAN AND AN EMPTY WHITE CUP

May 28, 2020

It is an unusual dream because it is about a person, I know, but I am not close to her. I quickly woke up and asked my husband if he could interpret the dream to me. I told Doug, "This is a dream of a person we know; her name is (No name will be mentioned for her privacy). Why am I dreaming about her?

Here is the dream: Walking through this woman's bedroom door I stood a slight distance from her bed. Her back was towards me and her face was toward the wall as she slept in her bed.

When she felt someone walking into her bedroom, she turned around from facing the wall and gently sat up on the edge of her bed.

She was wearing pajamas and I took notice of her perfectly styled hair. Observing her just sitting by the edge of her bed, I stood within the middle of this bedroom without moving for I was standing slightly before her.

The emotional vibe of this woman is a depressive state of mind. As she sat up on the edge of her bed, she motioned with her head and direct me to look of an empty white cup on a white saucer within the middle of her bedroom.

The white cup with its white saucer was in the center of her bedroom floor. It was totally empty with nothing inside of the white cup. She looked very depressed and filled with sorrow that the cup was totally empty (not a drop). I woke up as she was showing me the empty white cup.

Someone interpreted the dream for me and said, "The woman is thinking about what she does not have." Interestingly, I still did not understand as to why I dreamed about someone I see on occasions and as to why out of all the people I know would I be dreaming about this person? I later found out 'the why' of this dream. I will not reveal her personal details but it falls within the financial area. This dream bothered me so much that I wanted to run to the church and tell a priest, but I thought it was too crazy to mention it. So I just prayed about it. I am praying for this soul, now. Praying to God! I want something good to happen to this nice person very much!

Dr. Ronda's reflection:

We meet many people. We are very close only to some. The Holy Spirit seems to want me to respond to any person who looks sad by praying for them aloud if they talk about if or in my heart otherwise.

For you:

Why not pray for everyone you meet who seems depressed or sad?

Your thoughts or experiences:

Chapter Thirty-Five

DREAM OF THE SACRED HEART IMAGE AND THE OUR FATHER PRAYER SAVES ME ONE NIGHT!

August 05, 2020

his dream is about the Sacred Heart of Jesus and the power of the prayer of the Our Father Prayer for even the demons know "that at the name of Jesus every knee should bend, of those in heaven and on earth and under the earth and every tongue confess that Jesus Christ is Lord, to the glory of God the Father." (Philippians 2:10). The demons know that a slight glance at the image of Jesus Christ and the prayer that cries out to the Almighty shall overcome their wiles.

I got into my warm bed and fell asleep on my left side, where I am centered, with the Sacred Heart picture over the bed's headboard.

Now, take note as to the position I fell asleep and the location of the picture over my bed. In the dream, I was being held tightly by a person, who wrapped me so tight and in this same position I fell asleep in that I could not move at all. He was all dressed in black and could only see the face of the man. I have never seen this person. Intuitively, I was not scared in the dream for I knew to pray out loud with all of my heart.

Consistently, without any interruption I prayed the 'Our

Father' prayer out loud, as I remained in my position. The fully black coated person remained in his position. Now, I prayed the 'Our Father' even louder and did not stop praying the prayer out loud in my dream. I repeated it over and over again.

As I looked at this figure next to me, I was not scared, but upon looking at him, the figure started to sweat droplets on his face. So, I continued the 'Our Father' prayer and all I could see is sweat falling profusely from his face as he was next to me.

Then, the figure sat up and jumped out to the side of the bed. He stood up dressed in his long black coat and said to me, "I cannot stand this anymore!" I asked him, "Why can't you stand it?" He looked up towards the wall behind me and pointed to the wall to say, "Because of THAT!" He was drenching from the sweat falling all over his face. He turned from quickly from where he stood on the side of the bed and did not walk but ran to exit the bedroom door.

I woke up in the position I dreamt myself. Upon waking up, I turned around to see what he had pointed to and found it was the beautiful image of the 'Sacred Heart of Jesus,' that has been on the wall over my bed for twenty years.

The realization of the dream reminded me of the purpose to have sacred images around us. I would say the sweaty black figure who could not stand prayer represented evil turning into a man in the dream. My prayers of the 'Our Father' interrupted its plan because it could not stand the prayers and the wall image over my head of the Sacred Heart of Jesus.

I did wake up my husband after the dream but did not mention it to him. However, I asked him to pray with me the 'Divine Mercy' prayer for all souls. We prayed together.

A couple of days later, on a Sunday, I casually mentioned the dream to my husband and my son as we were having a conversation about the power of prayer. Devoting time for prayer such as the Our Father will make evil sweat and flee the premises. God is in everything!

Dr. Ronda's reflection:

I need to remember always to pray to the Sacred Heart of Jesus when I am anxious.

For you:

Try to do the same!

Your thoughts or experiences:

Chapter Thirty-Six
DREAM OF SNATCHING INNOCENT SOULS FROM DEMONS
August 07, 2021

The dream scared me so much that I immediately woke up my husband, Doug. I asked him to pray the rosary with me for all souls. Together, we prayed the rosary offering it up for all innocent souls that are suffering. I do not know what I meant by innocent souls but that is what I saw in my terrible dream. I will explain.

I found myself inside a home and within this home it was filled with the innocent being terrorized within this home. Inside were innocent people who were helpless. They had no help. So, I started to walk around the house to hear where all the loud crying was coming from. I walked into a room where demons were grabbing children (innocent souls) and throwing them around. They were scaring them with meanness and total ugliness.

The demons had long shaggy like hair and no clothing. One particular demon was extremely large with wide shoulders. I stood there and panicked because I could not believe what I was witnessing in the dream. Then they noticed and saw me looking at them. They yelled at me and cussed me out.

I started to pray the Hail Mary loud and the Our Father.

They grew agitated and came towards me. I told them, "I am here for them, and you are to give them to me, NOW!" They just kept tormenting the little ones and two of them approached me because I was a nuisance with my loud praying to the Blessed Mother, Mary. I recognized the home in my dream was not an ordinary home, it was a portal of evil that tormented babies.

I prayed louder and never stopped praying except to yell at them.

Suddenly, the two approached me and grabbed me along with another who was there to assist me. I was not allowed in the home or able to take the children (innocent souls) with us. So, I told the person that got throw out with me, "I will not leave until they give me all those souls. I am not leaving!"

I walked up the back porch stairs and through the screened back door and I started singing the "Ave Maria," and I also yelled out, "Ave Maria, Ave Maria over and over again."

All of the sudden I saw the back screen door and all the window screens of the home covered with a black blocking blind so I could not have any more viewing into the home.

However, one window gave me a slight access to view the inside of the home.

What I saw next was horrifying…I saw a demon throwing around the innocent souls from the neck. The ones I saw were infant children being taken out of their cribs.

I quickly left the backyard with the person next to me and walked around the sidewalk of the home. Finally, I stood in front of the home but on the outside of the property and fence (in other words the front sidewalk of the home).

I started yelling louder, "I am not leaving till you give them to me!"

I started praying the Hail Mary and the Our Father over and over and louder.

Finally, they got fed up with me and came outside with the souls. However, they were angrier than ever and one of them threw the souls over the fence to me and the other person that was with me. Then I saw the demons jumping over the fence, also. The other person that was with me quickly crossed the street, and I told the innocent souls, "Hurry, cross the street and follow him. Stay with him!"

The innocent souls all crossed over at that time.

The innocent's soul had crossed over and were all safe. All the demons left except for one, who grabbed me by the neck and was extremely angry. I did not give up and started even louder yelling, "Jesus Christ is King! Jesus rules over everything!" I started to pray the Our Father prayer. The demon could no longer look me in the face. He was dirty looking and the eyes were horrible. It turned its face because my praying was too much for it, as I prayed. It could not stand it!

Finally with my right hand I made a seal of the cross on my own forehead. Blessing myself while making the sign of the cross on my forehead by saying, "Father, Son and Holy Spirit" several times and it turned away from me. All the souls were finally saved at the end of my dream for they had crossed over to the other side.

I woke up! I was really terrified upon awakening and told my husband to hurry up, "We must pray the rosary quickly for the innocent souls needing prayers, now!"

I did go to confession later that day and was told it was a

spiritual warfare dream and to continue praying for souls for they need our assistance through prayer. So, when you pray say prayers for all souls, young and old for all need prayers.

Dr. Ronda's reflection:

I certainly found this dream scary! However, reading it triggered a fresh desire to pray unceasingly rebuking all evil spirits.

For you:

Look up spiritual warfare and choose a prayer to say yourself.

Your thoughts and experiences:

Chapter Thirty-Seven
DREAM OF A SOUL CONTENT IN MOVING ON

September 17, 2021

I woke up from a dream about someone I knew, a woman who was a great mother and wife. The reason I say 'I knew' is because she is no longer living or, better stated a deceased person who died from an illness.

The dream was of this woman sorting out shoes on a shoe shelf, except she could never finish putting up the shoes from shoe boxes on the shelf. The shoes would just multiply and multiply. The task would never be completed for the shoe boxes would just multiply as she tried putting them on the shelf. A difficult task, indeed!

I was on the other side of the tall shoe rack with another unknown person watching the woman trying so hard to do the job of putting up the shoes but to of no avail.

Then all the sudden I saw her just throw one of the shoes down. She made a motion with the hand, like I give up I am done and walked away from the shoe task. This person walked away by choice, freely, relieved, and so ready to move on.

After waking up, I looked up what shoes symbolize. They mean a new spiritual path or journey. I realized the woman whom I had not talked to in a decade, came to show me how she moved on from this life. Since, she recently passed away, it seemed she was very willingly, and made the decision on her own to not hold on but move on through the new spiritual journey with no regrets. She simply just decided to drop everything and just move on in spite of whatever. It did not matter because she was tired and chose to move on freely and not remain here. It was a choice not to continue fighting. She was content to have many paths or avenues as life offered to her, but through the frustration of consistent battles of health issues, it was easier to throw in the shoes and move on.

So, she dropped all the shoes and proceeded to walk, and kept on walking into her new journey again willingly, intentionally and would not look back and would not want to return to her former state in life. Interesting!

Dr. Ronda's reflection:

Analysts of dreams of the usual kind, which are not interior visions such as most of those Alicia tells us of, think that almost all images in dreams are symbolic of over fears and hopes. Whatever type of experience this is, Alicia's analysis seems true. We should let go of life if we are close to God when illness seems incurable. Not in the sense of euthanasia, but not clinging to extraordinary means to stay on earth. Check Catholic teaching on this if you don't understand what I mean.

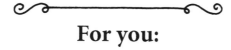

For you:

Are you eager to be with Jesus in heaven?

Your thoughts and experiences:

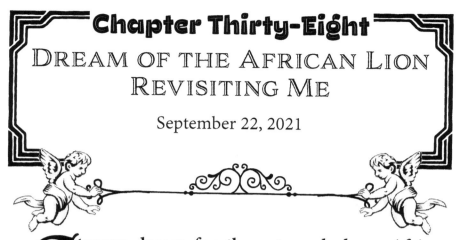

Chapter Thirty-Eight

DREAM OF THE AFRICAN LION REVISITING ME

September 22, 2021

Strange dream for the extremely large African lion comes back in to revisited me in this dream. In 2018, I dreamt feeding and walking side by side with a beautiful African lion. Now, four years later the African Lion comes back to my defense. How you ask, did this lion come to your defense? I will explain.

There was a black panther encircling me at a distance with a slow walking gait. He evil black panther with evil green eyes never removed his sight off me, as he is encircling and prowling around me. His head never flinched as he walked slowly the entire time. Helplessly, I sat petrified watching him encircling me.

Something unexpectedly happens as the black panther stood at a short distance from me. Suddenly, an extremely large tamed African lion reappears from a dream from several years ago in this dream, as he walks straight into my path where I was sitting down frightened of the panther. He walks directly across the area to come over to me to protect me.

The lion walks towards me to gently sit next to me. He places his extremely large head onto my chest. He never lifted his head up but found great comfort sitting right next to me with his head completely resting against my chest.

I began to pat the extremely large African lion gently on his head. I started to brush the lion's hair with my hand for he was a very tamed loving animal.

Being distracted by the African Lion, I now looked up to look for the panther. I now saw the panther no longer existed and was not within the premises at all. The evil panther had disappeared from the entire area as soon as the lion appeared within the area. Jesus, the Tribe of Judah came to protect me from evil in a dream. I woke up!

Dr. Ronda's reflection:

Oh, dear Jesus, Lion of Judah, do come and chase away any panther demons who threaten me!

For you:

Write your own prayer with your image of a panther and a lion.

Your thoughts or experiences:

Chapter Thirty-Nine
DREAM OF A STRUGGLING FAMILY
December 12, 2021

On Sunday's where I attend church, there is a great practicing Catholic with a wonderful family who was now in my dream on this night. I told my husband to please make a note of this date for it is a strange dream, because I feel something is going to happen to this family. So, I repeated the date to my husband, and he said, "Okay, I will remember the date." As strange as it sounds, I was relieved to know that he agreed to remember the date of the dream.

This is the dream…I dreamt, NO NAME looking around him as lost and worried about something. I could see his head turning from left to right in stress and anxiety. Then the dream changed to his wife.

I saw the wife carrying a large tote bag or purse on her shoulder. I saw an apple watch on her wrist as she was holding her large purse. Then in the dream, I see her twisting her wedding ring on her finger around in a nervous motion. She was twisting the ring around her finger with her other hand. This is where it gets strange, I see a total stranger coming towards her and stopping several feet from her as he pulls out a gun.

I woke up! I started to pray and thought why am I dreaming of people from church? If this dream means anything, what am I supposed to do with it, do I tell someone without sounding like a freak? So, I decided to tell my husband to remember the date in case something happens to this family. He agrees.

Well, a week later, December 19, 2021, at Sunday Mass we are sitting within the pews praying for the intentions of the Mass.

We heard in the petitions, "Pray for the (No Name) family. So, my husband and I quickly turned our heads to look at each other for they had announced the name of the family I dreamt about in the petitions. It had been on a couple of days since dreaming of this family.   I   told my husband to go find out what is going on after mass. He told me, "I am! I am going to ask." So, he knew the dream about this family is correct, but the content of the dream did not make any sense to us.

It turned out it was a family illness on December 14, 2021. I had the dream of the family on December 12, 2021. Again, I only see this nice family at Mass.

I believe in the power of prayer for all went well for the family through the action of prayer.

So, in this dream I felt there was a lot of confusion in the actions. I felt the content within the dream may not be totally correct but, somehow, I was picking up on people's emotions, 'after all we are all connected in one way or another.'

If you try to interpret the dream, as it leaves me to be puzzled, as for example, in seeing the wedding ring being twisted by the woman on her finger in a nervous manner may relate to anxiety, stress, or tension of their family situation. However, I could never figure out why I was dreaming about a gun. Maybe it was just showing a dangerous moment or even as a situation regarding someone's health. Who knows? It is a dream or vision into someone's else's life.

Upon seeing the man back at church, I told my husband I am going to tell him a few insights about the dream. So, we walked up to talk to the nice man.

I told him, "I had a dream about you." He looked stunned and said, "You dreamed about me!" I told him, "Yes, I did." I proceed to ask this person with a question, "We heard the intentions at Mass, is everything okay?" He answered, "Yes, my family member fell ill." So, I pushed it with another question, "When did your family member fall ill?" He answered me, "On December 14."

I was shocked and told him, "I dreamt you on December 12." He said, "On the day of Our Lady of Guadalupe." I quickly answered him, "Yes, on the day of Our Lady of Guadalupe."

So, I realized at that precise moment that on the night of the dream, prayers were needed for this family even if it was because of a dream or vision about them. Upon hearing this, I thought maybe the family member that fell ill or the person I spoke to about dreaming him must have a strong devotion to Our Lady of Guadalupe and has many graces.

Next, I hinted about his wife, as I told him, "Tell your wife not to carry such a large purse right now." He told me, "Why?" I thought to myself do not go to deep with this, so I said, "You know how it is people see large purses right now during the holidays and for safety during holidays I tell my daughters the same thing." I proceeded to tell him, "I tell them do not carry any large purses." He nodded in agreement.

At the following Sunday Mass, I inquired about the family member and was told all was well with the person.

Dr. Ronda's reflection:

I liked that Alicia hesitated before talking about the dream. It turned out well. I like the use of the word "seemed" often when I talk about "words" I get in prayer as in it seemed the Holy Spirit was telling me...

For you:

Do you have high intuition or dreams such as Alicia's?

Your thoughts or experiences:

Chapter Forty

DREAM THE SIN OF GLUTTONY REVEALS ITSELF

January 04, 2022

Perhaps there are times when God wants to **remind us of a sin,** one we did not realize the severity of it such as the sin of gluttony. For it brings so much damage to a person's entire body and the soul.

The night before the dream, a relative of mine went to confession and Mass after two years. It was great!

So, we did brunch earlier in the day at her request, I obliged since we would be having a wonderful evening. I extended an invitation for that evening to go to adoration, Mass and confession.

After evening Mass, both of us saw an old friend who had recently lost her mother. She invited both of us to a local restaurant and we all met at the restaurant. We reminisced about our good old gal days. It had been a couple of hours and it was now getting late, so we all went home.

Later, that night I fell asleep close to midnight to only find myself dreaming of the sin of gluttony coming to life.

In the dream, I saw plenty of beautiful painted ocean view apartments. They all had balconies on the outside of them. They were all high-rise apartments.

My apartment in the dream was the nicest one and on the very top of all the other apartments. However, the problem was all the other apartments' paint looked perfect with the only exception being my high-rise apartment. The paint was peeling even though it was supposed to be the nicest apartment. Yet it was not.

So, I was now inside the apartment. In the apartment, there was a large rectangular wooden table. I saw myself sitting in this wooden table eating from a large portioned plate.

I realized I was now looking at a dream of Gluttony. Gluttony, where food is so tantalizing but lacks the substance necessary to sustain the journey in life to eternity.

Dr. Ronda's reflection:

Most of us have some sins, faults, or defects we are in denial about. Perhaps, if less vivid than a warning in a dream such as Alicia's about gluttony, our wake-up call can be when someone dares to point out what we do wrong!

For you:

What is a sin or fault you need to admit to, confess, and pray to change?

Your thoughts or experiences:

GOD HAS A GREAT SENSE OF HUMOR! THE BEST!

I want to tell you that God does have a great sense of humor. How you ask? An experience I had when my children were in elementary. At the time, I told my husband I would like to buy a vehicle and he replied, "No, I do not think it is a good idea."

My reply to him while he sat there reading a book, "Fine, then I will ask God for the vehicle." Amusingly, he looked at me and told me, "Okay, fine! Go ahead! Ask Him!" and he went back to reading his book.

Honestly, I did just that as I prayed about getting a new vehicle. In prayer, I was specific and mentioned my wish for a nice car. As I prayed to God, I made it very specific and prayed the following, "God, I would like to ask you for something specific, a car. It needs to be affordable and if it could be new I would appreciate it. I will consider the car a gift from you."   The reason for asking for a car is because my husband had an excellent running vehicle but the air conditioning decide to no longer work in this car. My small kids one day told me, "Can we go buy a car right now before he gets home?" I thought what a funny thing to hear from children. I told them that was not the best idea, so I thought the solution was to pray about it.

So I did…

Well, a couple of weeks later, the phone rings and it is someone (No Name) calling me saying, "Alicia, I have a favor to ask you and Doug?" I never mention to anyone other than my husband about my prayer to God.

She told me, "I lost my job! I am unable to pay for my new

vehicle." And she continues to say, "Could you take the car? You can come over right now and take the car, it is yours! I just need someone to pay it, so I do not lose my credit." She stressed to me on the phone, "You do not need to give me any money at all. Just pick up the car, please." She did not want any money that she put into the vehicle as a down payment, it was "Just pick up the car!"

I took the receiver off my ear to looked up as she was speaking to me, "God if you can laugh you must be laughing at me really hard right now!" I can image you telling me, "I got you, now!" I was in total shock.

So, I spoke to my husband, and he said, "Yes, we will help her out." We went to pick up the keys and the car. It had less than one hundred miles and the auto dealer paper mats were still on the floor. We paid the car off for her and she kept her credit. I knew right there God listens to petitions, so this is a gift from God.

So, I went out and bought a huge sunflower with a pink ribbon, so it could be placed onto the back windshield of the vehicle, as I drove around town to remind me, the car was a gift from God. However, the greatest gifts we can ever have are the three theological virtues of the church: faith, hope and love.

Now, I wish to tell you about a recent high intuitive moment I recently had with (No Name). I will call this person, Jane.

Jane had been having a low-grade fever since January 24, 2022. She even went to the emergency room, where she had a low-grade fever. She was diagnosis with an infection, Pyelonephritis and given antibiotics to clear it up.

Days later, her low-grade fever returned even after a whole round of antibiotics, so she was given even more antibiotics, it would be her second round. However, she had alternating days of fever where some days her temperature was normal but during the evening her temperature was a low-grade fever during this next second round of antibiotics.

We prayed and worried about Jane.

Finally, I told Jane, "Can I come over so we can sit together to preview my book?" She said, "Yes, of course."

I took my laptop to her home. We sat there for three hours reading my book.

Next, Jane decides to go take her temperature. She tells me, "I have a low-grade fever of 99.9, I am on my second round of antibiotics." I told her, "Oh, no! That is way too many antibiotics."

All the sudden, I had a high intuitive moment! Unexpectedly and uncontrollably, the words rushed out of my mouth as I told her, "What if there is something wrong with the thermometer?" She replied, "What?" and said, "No way! I just bought this thermometer two months ago."

I told her, "No, there may be something wrong with the thermometer. Let's go to Walmart to get a thermometer. I will take you." She hesitated but agreed to go buy a thermometer.

She purchased a regular thermometer and a non-contact infrared thermometer. You will never guess! The first one, the non-contact infrared thermometer recorded normal temperature. So, she took her temperature with the new regular thermometer, it recorded a normal temperature. We were astonished and laughed like kids!

Next, she decided to take her temperature again and this time with the old thermometer. The old thermometer recorded a low-grade fever while the two new thermometers recorded no fever.

What a discovery!

My friend, Dr. Ronda Chervin told me, it is a spirit of charism. It showed up to guide me in helping Jane, so glad Jane listened to my intuitive moment. I realized all would be all right, as I asked Jane, "Which dream would you say is your favorite one?" Smiling and content with her state of life she says, "The Tree of Life."

Jane is now doing well.

Conclusion

These dreams or interior visions have continued today after sharing and writing the forty dreams I chose to write to you about in this book. For, I cannot choose as to how or when to dream this way, as it just happens when I fall asleep to only have the most profound dreams. So, I will keep writing them down and maybe there shall be a continuous book on interior visions. However, I wish to include and share two more of the latest dreams aside from the forty dreams, so consider these extra dreams for you to enjoy, here are two extras just for you!

Woke up to realize the dream dealt with clear rainwater dripping from a ceiling. But what puzzled me the most in this dream is the person whom the rainwater pours upon. Comfortably, sitting in a chair next to my husband, Doug who sits next to me in a chair viewing what looked to be a large event in the dream. There seems to be a lot of people in attendance at this event.

As we are sitting in this large area within a church, I feel water droplets falling from the ceiling land on me. It is the same for my husband, he feels and sees the droplets of water falling from the ceiling. It is clear rainwater, but it was not heavy or medium, it was very light drizzle of rain. I look up to the ceiling and find the water is coming from the ceiling and dripping on both of us.

Next, a couple of feet from my husband and myself, I see a Bishop sitting in a nice upholstered red chair with matching red vestments sitting comfortably in the red chair. He is facing the people, as he wears a white mitre.

Suddenly, I turn to look at the bishop to only see clear very heavy rainwater pouring onto the bishop and it is coming from the ceiling above him. Everything around him is dry except the bishop and the chair for the rain is non-stop and pouring upon him. He is completely drenched from the rainwater.

Now, I see myself with a folded white towel in my hand and standing by the bishop's chair. With the towel in my hands, I start to dry up the rain from the chair, as I circulate it around the chair to completely try to dry it. So, I am trying hard to wipe the chair down from the rain.

Then, the bishop tells me, "Don't worry about it. It is fine. It is okay." I look up to see him all dried up including his vestments along with the chair. Everything is completely dried up with no rainwater in sight. He is calm and peaceful. All is normal now.

The symbolism is amazing, so I looked up certain items or symbols from the dream on the Internet. The red chair signifies the chair as a throne, the bishop's *cathedra* is the seat of authority, the seat of the soul. The red chair in this dream symbolically may signify optimism and faith. The water is holy, a thirst for knowledge. It is a cleansing and renewal of the soul through spiritual activities such as for example, Baptism. This is what I dreamed one night.

A **very colorful dream! Being outside viewing torn down branches with plentiful of berries covering the tree branches** and also thrown throughout the green grass, I sat down by this tree with these berries. This tree had plentiful branches with these purplish colorful berries. I compare them to being plentiful as blueberries, but they are not blueberries for they look slightly different in color and size, for they seem to be larger than a blueberry.

Sitting comfortably in the grass, I start to remove the berries off the branches which had fallen onto the ground and patiently start to place the berries into the large white vessel or container. This large antique milk drum or wine container which at one time held liquids such as milk or wine. It is a large tall antique container. Suddenly, as I am picking up these berries, I turn my head over my shoulder slightly to take a quick glance of what is behind me.

I see an average size sleeping black cat that never moves a millimeter from a distance from the tree and myself. He is stretched out sleeping and is never awoken throughout the dream. All he did is sleep throughout the entirety of the dream without moving at all. So, I just turn my head back to the task at hand and continue enjoying picking all the berries off the branches to place them into this large antique wine or milk container.

So, I was happy and peaceful in this dream. I was joyful for there was an extreme abundance of these beautiful colorful berries.

Now, I completed filling up this white antique milk or wine container up the rim with these dark blue purplish berries. Remaining were some flexible branches without these berries since I already had taken out all the berries off them. So, what did I do next?

I gathered the branches without the berries and started to flex the branches. In flexing and molding the branches, I created a circle or a wreath since they were very flexible branches. The flexible branches with protruding small branches (thorny) out of it were well put together for they remained intact. I placed the wreath on top of all the loads of berries that were in the container. The wreath of the flexible branches with protruding branches rested on top of all these berries in the container.

So, what happened next? The filled up container is located to a different area by me as I take it by its handle to place it along a fence.

Suddenly, after placing the container down by the fence I look around to see plenty of people walking the area, for there is even people riding bicycles on this dirt path. There are no vehicles on site but only lots of people going about their business in this area. Then all of a sudden…

There is a young man within this crowd of people who stands out from the crowd of people. The young man across the street notices the container filled with berries and quickly walks towards me. He looks healthy, slender and strong.

The short wavy brown hair that parts in the middle seems to frame his face very well, as I notice his heavy wearing white wool tunic and light comfortable sandals. His complexion is clear with full brown wavy hair to the shoulders. The young man is filled with confidence as he walks towards me as he picks me in a crowd of people. He starts to walk towards me without any hesitation, as he crosses the dirt road and makes his way through the crowd of people.

As he approaches me, I immediately look at the young man to tell him, "Here, this container is for you" and I continue to tell him, "Here, take the container." The young man dressed in a white wool tunic does not hesitate for he nods his head in agreement, so I take the filled-up container with the berries and within the container lays the flexible wreath. I turn over the container to him, where he takes it by the two handles to carry the large antique wine or milk container. He is glad to have the antique container filled with berries, which contains a flexible wreath on top of all the berries laying within this container. The young man receives the container into his hands, as he receives it in a welcoming gesture of brotherly love. I woke up!

Now, I hope you have enjoyed the dreams, as for when we are awakening we are given the opportunity to reflect on prayer in calling out to God first, when we pray the rosary by announcing the three theological virtues of the Church, as we say the three Hail Mary's upon starting the rosary to say, "for faith, hope and charity." These three theological virtues of the church are immediately reflected upon praying the rosary, for we are immediately calling out to God, Our Father when we are announcing these three theological virtues of the Catholic church, again, as we declare in our rosary, "for faith, hope and charity." The continuation to pray the rosary after the announcement of the three theological virtues will give us a voice that God lovely listens to the intercession proceeded by our Blessed Mother, Mary Most Holy and Queen of Heaven and Earth, Mother of the Rosary, as we pray for petitions, our Church, vocations and all of our priest. The rosary is a gift to humanity. Never be disillusioned for Mary, Queen and Mother of the rosary will always intercede for us. Always! All we must do is pray and ask for her motherly intercession. God will take care of the rest, he always does even in dreams.

Concluding Prayer

Holy Spirit, may all my readers be enkindled by the light You have shed through these interior visions I call dreams.

About the Author

Alicia Harley, Mystic, Author and Writer of Spiritual Dreams for Our Journey to Eternity lives with her family in a beautiful Gulf coast city named after the Body and Blood of Christ, Corpus Christi, Texas. She has a Bachelor in English from Texas A&M-Corpus Christi. Currently, she has been meeting with a group of people in her home and continues group discussions consists of prayer and group interpretations on her dreams. She enjoys volunteering her time to evangelize about God to people living in a Living Facility and visits with them on a weekly basis. Alicia belongs to a Catholic organization, The Legion of Mary within the Catholic Diocese of Corpus Christi, Texas. She is a daily communicant at Holy Mass. She has been a Catholic Daughter Regent at the Cathedral. When her children were younger, she served on the Diocesan School Board representing a local Catholic school. Voluntarily, served for many years as an Altar Server Coordinator for the Corpus Christi Cathedral. Prior to Covid 19, she has served devoutly with a great love to God at his Holy Altar, as a Eucharistic Minister at the local Cathedral, Corpus Christi Cathedral. She hopes to continue writing more in the near future and teach people that dreaming in the spiritual world brings more faith, hope and charity among all of God's people and even those whom may choose to not believe, may find dreams interesting and want to worship God even more. For remember, God is in EVERYTHING, even in small things as dreams.

Made in the USA
Columbia, SC
14 February 2023

11970424R00139